The lament and imprecatory psalms are ofte
the church. In this highly readable book, M
rightly understood, they can be an importan
ral problem, namely, anger and unforgiven~~~. ~~~ ~~~p~~~~~~y ~~~~~~~~~~~~~~~
between righteous and unrighteous anger, between unconditional love and
conditional forgiveness. The result of a nuanced treatment of these emotionally charged topics is a book that will benefit anyone who struggles with these
issues. What makes it especially helpful is that it is grounded in the real life
encounters of the author as a pastor.

Rev. Simon Chan, PhD
Editor, *Asia Journal of Theology*
Former Lecturer in Theology,
Trinity Theological College, Singapore

In *God, I'm Angry!* Rev. Dr. Maggie Low tackles, with both competence and
compassion, thorny issues such as anger, unforgiveness, and vengeance. She
speaks as a theologian, exegeting numerous texts and engaging with selected
theologies. She speaks also as a pastor, drawing from her considerable experience in counselling believers. The case she makes goes against the grain of what
is often put forward as the biblical position on forgiveness. Whether we agree
with her or not, this book will not only push us to examine our personal stand,
it will also aid us in addressing this topic with greater clarity. I am pleased to
commend it to you.

Rt. Rev. Titus Chung, PhD
Bishop of The Anglican Church in Singapore

This is a courageous but timely book, delving into a topic that is seldom treated
and hence fraught with misunderstanding. Dr. Low is to be thanked for arguing strongly and clearly for a Christianity that is robust enough to take into its
ambit angry responses towards injustice and evil. While not all will agree with
her exegetical conclusions, they cannot deny that much food for thought has
been given. The many examples from her rich pastoral experience transport
the reader from mere academic discussion to the rough and tumble of life,
making this book particularly practical.

Tan Kim Huat, PhD
Chen Su Lan Professor of New Testament,
Trinity Theological College, Singapore

God, I'm Angry! manifests skilled Old Testament teacher Maggie Low's sensitivity and passion for attending to the pastoral needs of those she serves as she delves deeply into the psalms of vengeance. Her interest lies in more than just elucidating these very difficult psalms. Having encountered many who have experienced deep and unsettling feelings of anger, occasioned by all kinds of situations, she does not flinch from attending to these. She is prepared to disagree with accepted views that offer believers little or no help as they struggle with these raw emotions.

Maggie's writing is easily accessible, and her desire to see her readers move in a direction that will enable them to participate in behaviour that is pleasing to their Father in heaven is clear to see in this book.

Joseph John
Adjunct Lecturer,
School of Counselling, Singapore Bible College

How should we handle the anger we feel when we are sinned against and hurt by others? Some (consciously) suppress the anger and suffer from physical ill-health. Others (unconsciously) repress the anger and suffer emotionally. Yet others give vent to their anger by freely expressing it, which is often unhelpful. The key is to learn to process the anger in God's presence. The final chapter of Dr. Maggie Low's thoughtful book is particularly helpful in this regard. It provides help for sufferers as well as pastoral counsellors.

Bishop Emeritus Robert Solomon, PhD
The Methodist Church in Singapore

God, I'm Angry!

Langham
GLOBAL LIBRARY

God, I'm Angry!

Anger, Forgiveness, and the Psalms of Vengeance

Maggie Low

© 2023 Maggie Low

Published 2023 by Langham Global Library
An imprint of Langham Publishing
www.langhampublishing.org

Langham Publishing and its imprints are a ministry of Langham Partnership

Langham Partnership
PO Box 296, Carlisle, Cumbria, CA3 9WZ, UK
www.langham.org

ISBNs:
978-1-83973-685-8 Print
978-1-83973-770-1 ePub
978-1-83973-771-8 Mobi
978-1-83973-772-5 PDF

British Library Cataloguing-in-Publication Data
A catalogue record for this book is available from the British Library

ISBN: 978-1-83973-685-8

Cover & Book Design: projectluz.com

Contents

Abbreviations

AB	Anchor Bible
ABC	Asia Bible Commentary
BCOTWP	Baker Commentary on the Old Testament Wisdom and Psalms
BDB	Brown, Francis, S. R. Driver, and Charles A. Briggs. *A Hebrew and English Lexicon of the Old Testament*
BECNT	Baker Exegetical Commentary on the New Testament
BST	Bible Speaks Today
FOTL	Forms of the Old Testament Literature
JSOTSup	Journal for the Study of the Old Testament Supplement Series
NAC	New American Commentary
NCB	New Century Bible
NIBCOT	New International Biblical Commentary on the Old Testament
NICNT	New International Commentary on the New Testament
NICOT	New International Commentary on the Old Testament
NIGTC	New International Greek Testament Commentary
NIVAC	NIV Application Commentary
PNTC	Pillar New Testament Commentary
SHBC	Smyth and Helwys Bible Commentary
Smyth	Smyth, Herbert Weir. *Greek Grammar*. Revised by Gordon M. Messing. Cambridge: Harvard University Press, 1956.
SNTSMS	Society for the New Testament Studies Monograph Series
TDOT	*Theological Dictionary of the Old Testament*. Edited by G. Johannes Botterweck and Helmer Ringgren. Translated by John T. Willis et al. 8 vols. Grand Rapids: Eerdmans, 1974–2006.
TOTC	Tyndale Old Testament Commentary
WBC	Word Biblical Commentary

Introduction
and Acknowledgements

Y ou get angry, and then you feel guilty for being angry. Sound familiar?
Jesus said that anger is as sinful as murder, didn't he? So you try to
forgive your enemy, but you feel so upset by the injustice. You struggle to say
as Jesus did at the cross, "Father, forgive them, for they know not what they
do." But you still get triggered or end up numbing yourself and trying to ignore
psychosomatic symptoms like insomnia and indigestion.

Christians have been conditioned by well-meaning presumptions about
anger and forgiveness, but are such beliefs the biblical truths? We might know
how to do sadness with God because it's OK not to be OK. After all, the psalmist
lamented, "Why are you cast down, O my soul . . . ?" (Ps 42:5). But we hardly
hear anything about doing anger with God or about the psalmist who cursed
his enemies, "O God, break the teeth in their mouths," "Break the arm of the
wicked" (Pss 58:6; 10:15).

This book helps you express and resolve your hurts and anger by bringing
them to God through the imprecatory psalms – that is, psalms that call for
vengeance. We will see what the Bible really teaches about anger and forgiveness,
and, where necessary, we will learn about the texts in their original languages.

You will discover that anger can be a force for good and that Jesus never
taught us to forgive *unconditionally*. He does, however, command us to *love*
our enemies unreservedly. Forgiveness is commanded only when there is
repentance, and such conditional forgiveness is based on God's own example
in the Old Testament (OT) and the New Testament (NT).

Where there is no repentance, Romans 12:19 tells us, "Beloved, never
avenge yourselves, but leave room for the wrath of God; for it is written,
'Vengeance is mine, I will repay, says the Lord.'" In the Scripture, vengeance
and enemy love go hand in hand.

The psalms of vengeance show us how to bring our anger and desire for
retribution to God; but can Christians pray curses on enemies? Theologians
have suggested many ways of dealing with these violent psalms. I propose that
they are best understood in the light of OT concepts such as creation, covenant
(Abrahamic, Mosaic, Davidic), and Zion theologies. We will take an in-depth
look at Psalms 83, 109, and 137 to learn about these theological foundations.

The chapters on these three psalms are more exegetically rigorous, so the busy reader might want to skip ahead to the theological analysis at the end of each chapter. When you need to use the psalms, you can return for a closer study. It will be seen that God is a God of both relentless grace and unrelenting justice.

The last chapter, "Ministering with the Psalms of Vengeance," shows you how to apply these truths to your own life and equips you to counsel others. Often, even pastors do not know what to say to troubled people beyond "I will pray for you." This chapter was the blueprint for an assignment in my course on the imprecatory psalms. Participants found volunteers to be their counsellees and prayerfully took them through the steps. The students reported that they were able to minister more meaningfully and that their friends could begin a journey of healing. You, too, can learn to use the lament and imprecatory psalms as instruments of growth and liberation. I include real-life testimonies as encouraging demonstrations of God's power at work in his people.

Below, I acknowledge all those who bravely signed up for my course on the imprecatory psalms in 2021. Their questions and contributions helped to sharpen my thinking and clarify my writing.

Amelia Stanley	Gladys Zhong
Amos Chan	Ho Shwu Ling
Amos Yeo	Mark Lim
Celest Cheong	Nguyen Kim Chau
Chang Chong Tian	Ong Bee Keow
Dorothy Koh	Paulo Caperig
Elena Yeo	Tan Bong Loo
Eliza Poh	Tham Wen Chen
Gao Yuhan	Wennie Dong

I thank Trinity Theological College for my six-month sabbatical leave in 2020 to research and draft this book. I am grateful for my colleague, Dr. Tan Kim Huat, who shared his expertise in the NT with me, although any shortcomings are mine alone. Above all, I thank my husband, David, and my children, Micah and Melissa, for graciously giving me the space and time to write. This is the second book on my bucket list that God planted in my heart, and I believe that is because he wants to speak to you, dear reader.

1

Is It OK to Be Angry?

Clenching his teeth, Andy[1] prayed, "Lord, I forgive him!"

"Hold on, Andy," I said. "Can you first tell God how angry you are with your boss?" Andy remained mute, brows furrowed. "It's OK. God understands," I coaxed.

This conversation took place after I preached at a church service. Andy had come to ask me a theological question: "Why does God allow bad things to happen to his people?" I was surprised because the question was unrelated to my sermon. Sensing a personal issue, I asked the reason for his question. Then he poured out his troubles: a new boss who blamed him for everything and criticized him in public. Andy said it was even more infuriating because the boss claimed to be a Christian but didn't act like one. He felt so belittled that he wanted to quit his job but he worried about supporting his family.

I offered to pray with him, and that's when he spat out the words, "Lord, I forgive him!" Like many good Christians, Andy felt that he shouldn't be angry, even when wronged and hurt. Besides, he was a church leader and probably thought he should demonstrate a "good" Christian attitude. But those words couldn't mask his anger.

So I interrupted and invited him to tell God his real feelings. I waited while he struggled to express his frustrations, but when he did, tears came trickling down. After I took him through the process of prayer (see ch. 11), his face radiated with peace.

Most faithful churchgoers believe that anger is sinful and should be suppressed. Any psychologist would tell you that refusing to admit your feelings doesn't make them go away; they lie buried, usually leading to psychosomatic problems. Some people explode by taking their feelings out on others, while

---

1. Names and details have been changed to protect the privacy of all individuals in this book.

1

others implode and take them out on themselves, resulting in depression. Besides, as Federico G. Villanueva points out, it is hypocritical to pray blessing for someone when we feel angry and don't mean what we say.[2]

What does the Bible say about anger? We will look at five examples of rage in the OT, with a more extensive discussion of six NT texts that seem to imply anger is a sin. A proper interpretation will show that anger as an emotion is not wrong; instead, we need to look at why we get angry and what we do with it.

Anger in the OT

The word "anger" in the OT translates fourteen Hebrew words, with *'aph* and *khemah* occurring most often. *'Aph* means "nose" and is related to the verb *'anaph*, "to snort," which is a physical expression of anger. *Khemah* means "heat," another metaphor for anger. The NRSV uses "anger" 322 times in the Bible, with an overwhelming number referring to God's wrath. The word "angry" occurs 118 times, of both God and people. Human anger in the OT may or may not be justified. Here, I highlight five occasions where human outrage was entirely legitimate: these incidents involve Moses, Saul, David, Jonathan, and Nehemiah.

1. Moses in Exodus 32:19

> As soon as he came near the camp and saw the calf and the dancing, Moses' *anger* burned hot, and he threw the tablets from his hands and broke them at the foot of the mountain.[3]

In Exodus 32, God himself was angry with the people and wanted to destroy them because they had rejected God by worshipping a golden calf. Moses's shattering of the law tablets demonstrated that the covenant was irreparably broken. His fury reflected God's own anger with the use of the same Hebrew phrase "*kharah 'aph*" (literally, to burn or kindle one's nose). This phrase occurs

---

2. Federico G. Villanueva, *It's OK to Be Not OK: Preaching the Lament Psalms* (Carlisle: Langham Preaching Resources, 2017), 84.

3. All Scripture citations are from the NRSV, unless otherwise indicated. All emphasis in Scripture citations is added.

five times in this chapter: three times with regard to God (32:10, 11, 12) and twice for Moses (32:19, 22).[4]

2. Saul in 1 Samuel 11:6

And the spirit of God came upon Saul in power when he heard these words, and his *anger* was greatly kindled.

Saul was provoked by the Ammonites' threat to gouge out the right eye of every Israelite in Jabesh-gilead. His anger was kindled by the spirit of God to fight for the people. Anger is the proper response to threats and injustice.

3. Jonathan in 1 Samuel 20:34

Jonathan rose from the table in fierce *anger* and ate no food on the second day of the month, for he was grieved for David, and because his father had disgraced him.

King Saul had tried to kill David by hurling a spear at him. Saul's son Jonathan was enraged because the king broke his promise not to kill David. Jonathan then risked everything to protect David, recognizing that David was God's chosen king (1 Sam 23:17). His anger was aligned with God's purpose and saved an innocent victim.

4. David in 2 Samuel 12:5

Then David's *anger* was greatly kindled against the man. He said to Nathan, "As the LORD lives, the man who has done this deserves to die."

David was reacting to Nathan's story about a wealthy fellow who slaughtered a poor man's lamb. The king did not realize that it was a parable of his adultery

---

4. Moses's actions in Exod 32:20 where he burned the idol, ground it to powder, scattered it on the water, and made the Israelites drink it, seems excessively punitive. However, it needs to be understood as an ancient practice of destroying idols. The Ugaritic god of death, Mot, was burned, ground, and scattered by the goddess Anat, becoming food for the birds. King Josiah carried out a similar act with the Asherah idols in 2 Kgs 23:6. Douglas K. Stuart writes that, by making people drink the crushed idol, Moses ensured that it "came out as waste, corrupted and defiled, and therefore was ruined permanently as material fit for an idol" (*Exodus*, NAC [Nashville: Broadman & Holman, 2006], 678). So also William H. C. Propp, *Exodus 19–40*, AB (New York: Doubleday, 2006), 560.

with Bathsheba and the subsequent murder of her husband. His angry reaction was right in wanting justice for the poor man. Although he said that the offender deserved to die, he acted in accordance with the law and pronounced the sentence that the wrongdoer should restore the lamb fourfold (Exod 22:1). Thus, when Nathan responded to David by saying, "You are the man," the king was immediately convicted of his sin and God's punishment was seen as just.

5. Nehemiah in Nehemiah 5:6

I was very *angry* when I heard their outcry and these complaints.

Nehemiah was furious when he realized that the affluent elites were oppressing their poor countrymen. In the next verse, Nehemiah carefully pondered the problem before he acted. His reflection shows what righteous anger looks like: it should goad us to act, but in wisdom. So, Nehemiah called for a public meeting where he emphasized that the people should be empathetic to one another, fear God, and be a testimony to their enemies. He also admitted his own wrong and set the example by restoring everything to the debtors. Thus, the conflict was resolved.

The above examples may give the impression that righteous anger comes only in the context of defending others. However, the imprecatory psalms express anger against enemies who attacked the psalmists themselves. Psalm 55, for example, asks God to punish the psalmist's "frenemy" – a close friend who had turned against him (Ps 55:12–15).

Thus, one can be angry for the right reasons and respond with the right actions. A couple of other accounts show that even when a person reacted out of anger without just cause, God did not condemn but merely guided the person in his or her reflection. The first person in the Bible to get angry was Cain because God had accepted his brother's offering but not his.[5] To this reaction, God merely asked Cain why he was angry and directed him to do the right thing (Gen 4:6–7). Divine punishment was imposed only after Cain committed fratricide. Jonah is another case in point. When he was angry that God did not destroy the Ninevites as prophesied, God only asked him, "Is it right for you to be angry?" (Jonah 4:4). The Creator then proceeded to teach him compassion.

---

5. This was probably due to Abel offering the "firstlings" of his flock, while Cain brought an offering of "fruit" rather than firstfruits (Gen 4:3–4) – i.e. Cain did not offer his best to God, while Abel did.

There may be times when anger is an instinctive reaction, and the justification may not be immediately apparent. Was the driver who crashed into your car drunk, or was he having a heart attack? Were you chided by your boss because he was biased or because you made a mistake? Emotions are not sinful in themselves, but we would do well to take the Nehemiah approach: to think over the matter before acting (Neh 5:7).

Anger in the NT

Despite these OT examples, Christians find it hard to shake off the belief that anger is a sin, primarily because Jesus likened anger to murder (Matt 5:22). However, Paul exhorted the church to be angry but not sin (Eph 4:26).[6] The Greek *noun* for anger, *orgē*, is used thirty-six times in the NT, with only five references to human anger (Eph 4:31; Col 3:8; 1 Tim 2:8; Jas 1:19, 20).[7] We will examine three didactic texts that raise questions about anger (Matt 5:22; Eph 4:26; and Jas 1:19),[8] followed by another three narratives where Jesus showed anger.

1. Jesus's Sermon on the Mount (Matt 5:21–26)

> [21] You have heard that it was said to those of ancient times, "You shall not murder"; and "whoever murders shall be liable to judgment." [22] But I say to you that if you are angry with a brother or sister, you will be liable to judgment; and if you insult a brother or sister, you will be liable to the council; and if you say, "You fool," you will be liable to the hell of fire. [23] So when you are offering your gift at the altar, if you remember that your brother or sister has something against you, [24] leave your gift there before the altar and go; first be reconciled to your brother or sister, and then come

---

6. The Greek verb for anger (*orgizō* in the active/*orgizesthe* in the passive) is used eight times in the NT, all referring to human anger. It is used three times in three parables where the enraged person represents God and the anger would, thus, be righteous anger. It is used another three times for the unrighteous anger of the elder brother in the parable of the prodigal son, the rebellious nations in Rev 11:18, and the dragon in Rev 12:17. The last two occurrences of the verb are found in Jesus's teaching in Matt 5:22 and Paul's exhortation in Eph 4:26.

7. Harold W. Hoehner, *Ephesians: An Exegetical Commentary* (Grand Rapids: Baker Academic, 2002), 619, 635.

8. 1 Tim 2:8 is not discussed because it associates anger with argument, implying a contentious attitude.

and offer your gift. [25] Come to terms quickly with your accuser while you are on the way to court with him, or your accuser may hand you over to the judge, and the judge to the guard, and you will be thrown into prison. [26] Truly I tell you, you will never get out until you have paid the last penny.

Is Jesus saying that any anger is a sin as grave as murder? A closer look will show that Jesus is referring to a much more grievous attitude.

First, the Greek verb translated as "angry" in 5:22 is a present participle (*orgizomenos*), indicating a continuous action. It is better translated as "continuously angry" or "keeps on being angry."[9] Thus, this is not a momentary flash of anger but one that is kept simmering and brewing.

Second, the comparison to murder in 5:21 implies an anger that desires the destruction of another. As Donald A. Hagner says, it may be described as "murdering your brother in your heart."[10] After all, when Jesus discussed lust in Matthew 5:27–30, he said it is equivalent to committing adultery in one's heart, implying that the offence is not a passing thought or look but an intentional mental act.[11] So also for anger, the problem is not the emotional reaction but a sustained antagonism.

That this is contemptuous anger is, third, shown by the verbal insults thrown at the other in 5:22.[12] While God prohibited murder in Genesis 9:6 on the basis that all humans are made in God's image, Jesus extended that principle not just to how one acts but also to how one thinks and speaks to another person. To insult another is to undermine that individual's God-given worth and honour, making the insulter liable to God's judgment.[13] This attack hurts the other person so that he or she has "something against you" (5:23),

---

9. Andrew D. Lester, *The Angry Christian: A Theology for Care and Counseling* (Louisville: Westminster John Knox, 2003), 143; Carl G. Vaught, *The Sermon on the Mount: A Theological Investigation*, rev. ed. (Waco: Baylor University Press, 2001), 64. There are two other occurrences of the participle's usage in the NT: Matt 18:34 and Luke 14:21; but both refer to God's anger.

10. Donald A. Hagner, *Matthew 1–13*, WBC (Dallas: Word, 1993), 116.

11. John Nolland, *The Gospel of Matthew*, NIGTC (Grand Rapids: Eerdmans, 2005), 237, argues that natural sexual desire is not criticized but the indulgence of illicit sexual activity in the realm of the imagination.

12. So also R. T. France, *Matthew*, NICNT (Grand Rapids: Eerdmans, 2007), 201. Hagner, *Matthew 1–13*, 116, also notes that name-calling was a much more serious offence in biblical times because of the importance attached to one's name.

13. Nolland, *Matthew*, 234; Robert H. Gundry, *Matthew: A Commentary on His Literary and Theological Art* (Grand Rapids: Eerdmans, 1982), 87, says that such unrelenting anger and animosity "falsifies profession of discipleship."

for which "you" (the angry person) are instructed to make amends before coming to the altar.[14]

Fourth, a text-critical study shows that early readers had difficulty with this absolute injunction against anger. A strong manuscript tradition adds the phrase "without cause" in 5:22: "But I say to you that if you are angry with a brother or sister *without cause*, you will be liable to judgment." Craig L. Blomberg believes that while this addition is late, it gives the correct interpretation because there is a place for righteous indignation against sin.[15]

The fifth and final point is to consider the canonical context. Jesus himself displayed anger when he drove out the merchants and money-changers in the temple (Matt 21:12). The same word for anger (*orgē*) is used regarding Jesus's reaction to the Pharisees in Mark 3:5. In fact, Jesus also used the same term "fool" (*mōros*) for the Pharisees (Matt 23:17) and those who do not obey his words (Matt 7:26). While we need to be careful with our words, there may be occasions when the label is appropriate.[16]

First John 3:15, "All who hate a brother or sister are murderers," echoes Jesus's teaching by using Cain as the example (1 John 3:12). Cain's killing of his brother was not a rash act of anger, but was carried out with malicious planning, evident by Cain asking Abel to go out into the field so that they could be alone (Gen 4:8). Jesus was not talking about an emotional reaction but a hatred that deliberately causes hurt. Therefore, not all anger is wrong, and in fact, Paul commands us to get angry in Ephesians 4:26.

2. A Command to Be Angry (Eph 4:25–32)

[25] Therefore, putting away lying, "Let each one of you speak truth with his neighbor," for we are members of one another. [26] "Be angry, and do not sin": do not let the sun go down on your wrath, [27] nor give place to the devil. [28] Let him who stole steal no longer,

14. Craig L. Blomberg, *Matthew*, NAC (Nashville: Broadman & Holman, 1992), 107, makes the practical point that we cannot guarantee that the other person will agree to be reconciled with us, but we should make every effort to do so. The issue of forgiveness is addressed in ch. 3 in relation to the Lord's Prayer.

15. Blomberg, *Matthew*, 106. Blomberg refers to Jesus's and God's righteous anger in Matt 21:12–17; 18:34; 22:7. Ulrich Luz, *Matthew 1–7*, A Continental Commentary, trans. Wilhelm C. Linns (Minneapolis: Fortress, 1989), 284, cites the first-century pseudepigraphic book of 2 Enoch that "he who expresses anger to any person without provocation will reap anger in the great judgment" (44:2). However, Lester, *Angry Christian*, 143, warns that a "cause" does not justify all kinds of anger, such as revenge, jealousy, bitterness, or a long-standing resentment.

16. Blomberg, *Matthew*, 107.

but rather let him labor, working with his hands what is good, that he may have something to give him who has need. ²⁹ Let no corrupt word proceed out of your mouth, but what is good for necessary edification, that it may impart grace to the hearers. ³⁰ And do not grieve the Holy Spirit of God, by whom you were sealed for the day of redemption. ³¹ Let all bitterness, wrath, anger, clamor, and evil speaking be put away from you, with all malice. ³² And be kind to one another, tenderhearted, forgiving one another, even as God in Christ forgave you. (NKJV)

The crux here is whether the Greek imperative *orgizesthe* ("be angry") in 4:26 is a command. Some commentators tone it down by taking the imperative as conditional ("*if* you do get angry").[17] However, three factors will show that *orgizesthe* should be understood as a command: (1) Paul's use of Psalm 4:4, (2) the context of Ephesians 4, and (3) the syntax of the verse.

First, the phrase "Be angry, and do not sin" is an exact citation of the LXX (Greek Septuagint) of Psalm 4:4. The context of the psalm will help us understand the command better.

Psalm 4
To the leader: with stringed instruments. A Psalm of David.
¹ Answer me when I call, O God of my right!
    You gave me room when I was in distress.
    Be gracious to me, and hear my prayer.
² How long, you people, shall my honour suffer shame?
    How long will you love vain words, and seek after lies?
    Selah
³ But know that the LORD has set apart the faithful for himself;
    the LORD hears when I call to him.
⁴ When you are disturbed [Hebrew *ragaz*; Greek *orgizesthe*],
    do not sin;
    ponder it on your beds, and be silent. *Selah*
⁵ Offer right sacrifices,
    and put your trust in the LORD.
⁶ There are many who say, "O that we might see some good!

17. Andrew T. Lincoln, *Ephesians*, WBC (Dallas: Word, 1990), 300, takes the concessive view, saying that this text is not giving permission to get angry. Daniel B. Wallace, "ΟΡΓΙΖΕΣΘΕ in Ephesians 4:26: Command or Condition?," *Criswell Theological Review* 3, no. 2 (1989): 357, writes that there is no need to distinguish between permissive ("be angry if you must"), concessive ("although you may get angry"), and conditional ("if you get angry").

Let the light of your face shine on us, O LORD!"
[7] You have put gladness in my heart
   more than when their grain and wine abound.
[8] I will both lie down and sleep in peace;
   for you alone, O LORD, make me lie down in safety.

In the LXX of Psalm 4:4, the Hebrew imperative *ragaz* is translated into the Greek imperative *orgizesthe*. However, *ragaz* literally means "tremble" and can refer to shaking out of fear, awe, or anger.[18] In the context of Psalm 4, it is better understood as shaking in awe of God because the psalmist has said that the LORD hears him (4:3), and so his foes should tremble and not sin (4:4).[19]

In contrast, Greek readers of Psalm 4 would have to understand *orgizesthe* as David telling his *own* men to be angry with the enemies' vain words and lies (4:2). The Greek understanding is behind Ephesians 4:25–26, where the command to be angry follows the prohibition against lies.[20]

Second, the context of Ephesians 4:25–32 consists of five practical instructions arising from being a new person in Christ (4:20–24). As Harold W. Hoehner points out, each exhortation has three parts: (1) a negative command, (2) a positive command, and (3) the reason for the positive command.[21] Since all the other positive exhortations are understood as commands ("speak" in 4:25; "work" in 4:28; "proceed" in 4:29;[22] and "be kind" in 4:32), it follows that "be angry" is also a command.[23]

---

18. רגז, BDB, 919.

19. All four other uses of *ragaz* in the Psalms (Pss 18:8; 77:17, 19; 99:1) are of nature and people trembling in awe because of God. Wallace, "Ephesians 4:26," notes that the Targum and Aquila opt for "tremble [in fear/reverence]."

20. While "Be angry, and do not sin" may have become a proverbial statement in Paul's time (Wallace, "Ephesians 4:26," 359), the verbal and contextual echoes from Psalm 4 add to the likelihood that the imperative of *orgizesthe* was understood as a command.

21. Hoehner, *Ephesians*, 614. An exception is the second command about anger in 4:26, which begins with a positive command before stating the negative. Although Hoehner does not explain the reversal, we can see that it was due to Paul's verbatim citation of Ps 4:4.

22. "Proceed" in 4:29 does double duty for the negative and positive mandates.

23. This command may seem to contradict Eph 4:31, "Put away from you bitterness, wrath, anger [*orgē*], clamor, and evil speaking, with all malice." However, *orgē* has to be interpreted in context, since it may be taken positively or negatively. The list in 4:31 shows that it refers to malicious anger in contrast to the kindness and forgiveness mandated in 4:32 (Hoehner, *Ephesians*, 620; Wallace, "Ephesians 4:26," 363).

However, even legitimate anger needs to be processed in a timely way: "Do not let the sun go down on your wrath [*parorgismos*]."[24] Interestingly, Paul adds the prepositional prefix *para* to the noun *orgē* in this verse. This rare word occurs only once in the NT but seven times in the LXX for rebellious acts that brought God's judgment.[25] Thus, Paul is concerned that anger should not lead to wrong actions.

The third point has to do with Greek syntax. If "be angry" is a conditional imperative, then the general rule is that a conditional imperative would be followed by a future indicative rather than another imperative. For example, John 2:19 says, "Destroy [conditional imperative] this temple, and in three days I will [future indicative] raise it up." However, this sequence would not make sense in Ephesians 4:26 because it would be rendered as "If you are angry [conditional imperative], you will not sin [future indicative]." Thus Daniel Wallace concludes that Ephesians 4:26 is a command, putting a moral obligation on believers to be angry when necessary.[26]

Wallace explains that not giving place to the devil in 4:27 means, "Don't let the devil gain a foothold in the assembly by letting sin go unchecked."[27] This interpretation is apt, since Paul's emphasis in Ephesians is on being members of one body. Thus, the command is to be angry with what causes harm to the community.[28] In his commentary on this verse, John Stott tells Christians that "in the face of blatant evil we should be indignant not tolerant, angry not apathetic. . . . If evil arouses his anger, it should arouse ours also."[29] However, James seems to have a negative view of anger in his epistle, and to that we now turn.

---

24. As to whether this injunction should be taken literally, Hoehner, *Ephesians*, 621, recognizes it as a proverb mentioned by Plutarch. Thus, it is good counsel to follow in spirit rather than legalistically.

25. Hoehner, *Ephesians*, 621, gives the example of Manasseh's provocation of the Lord (2 Kgs 23:26; cf. also 1 Kgs 15:30; 2 Kgs 19:3; Neh 9:18, 26; Pss Sol 8:9). Jer 21:5 uses it in the passive sense for God's anger.

26. Wallace, "Ephesians 4:26," 370–72. Wallace conducted a study of all 187 constructions of imperative + *kai* (and) + imperative in the NT. Excluding Eph 4:26, he found only four possibilities (John 1:46; 7:52; 11:34; Luke 7:7) of reading the first imperative as a condition, but it would require the second imperative to function as a future indicative; e.g. John 1:46, "Come and see," has to be understood as "Come, and you will see."

27. Wallace, "Ephesians 4:26," 365, followed by Clinton E. Arnold, *Exegetical Commentary on the New Testament* (Grand Rapids: Zondervan, 2010), 301.

28. Wallace, 365, n. 70, proposes that *orgizō* tends to accent the volition, while *thymoō* (wrath, rage) tends to stress the emotion.

29. John R. W. Stott, *The Message of Ephesians: God's New Society*, BST (Downers Grove: InterVarsity Press, 1979), 186.

3. A Command to Be Slow to Anger (Jas 1:19–20)

[19] You must understand this, my beloved: let everyone be quick to listen, slow to speak, slow to anger; [20] for your anger does not produce God's righteousness.

James 1:20 appears to regard all human anger negatively. The verse needs to be explained according to its proverb genre and the historical context of the epistle. Here, James is referring to a selfish kind of anger.

First, James is citing from various OT and intertestamental writings, with Proverbs 17:27–28 being a prime example, especially as it advocates restraining one's words and anger:

> One who spares words is knowledgeable;
>   one who is cool in spirit has understanding.
> Even fools who keep silent are considered wise;
>   when they close their lips, they are deemed intelligent.

Douglas Moo argues that James is not prohibiting all kinds of anger because the nature of the wisdom genre is to make assertions that are generally but not always true.[30] That is, while anger usually causes one to act rashly, there may be circumstances when it is necessary (as in Eph 4:26 above). Furthermore, the sages present the truth as a contrast between two ways of life: righteousness versus wickedness. Similarly, James 1:20 contrasts human unrighteous anger and God's righteousness.[31]

Second, James's historical context explains what kind of anger he was concerned with: strife between rich and poor (5:1–6), which leads people to curse (3:10), slander (4:11), and even kill (4:2) one another. As Scot McKnight says, James is not concerned with mere frustration, but anger that leads to violence,[32] born out of greed.

Even so, the fact that James instructs to be slow to anger rather than to stop being angry shows that anger as an emotion is not wrong in itself. Rather, it is when such anger leads to sinful attitudes and actions that it becomes a problem. While an unfair situation may provoke an angry reaction, we need to slow down and reflect on whether it has to do with our covetous desires (1:14)

---

30. Douglas J. Moo, *The Letter of James*, PNTC (Grand Rapids: Eerdmans, 2000), 84. In fact, there are contradictory sayings within the book of Proverbs itself, leaving the reader to think about the appropriate application in different settings. An example is Prov 26:4–5 where one is told both to answer and not to answer a fool.

31. Luke Timothy Johnson, *The Letter of James*, AB (New York: Doubleday, 1995), 205.

32. Scot McKnight, *The Letter of James*, NICNT (Grand Rapids: Eerdmans, 2011), 138.

or because we truly want to defend the needy. The latter, says James, is what true religion is about (1:27). Thus, the anger that James is against in 1:20 is not just any kind of outrage but an egotistic temper that tears others down.[33]

Having looked at the three didactic texts on anger, we now turn to three narratives where Jesus felt, acted, and spoke in fierce displeasure.

4. Healing of a Man with a Withered Hand (Mark 3:5)

> He looked around at them with anger; he was grieved at their hardness of heart and said to the man, "Stretch out your hand." He stretched it out, and his hand was restored.

There are two emotions that Jesus felt: anger and grief. Robert H. Gundry distinguishes between the causes of these reactions. He points out that Jesus sorrowed specifically over his enemies' hardness of heart, for that hardness would work out to their detriment. His anger, however, was at their refusal to help others, as they remained silent despite his challenge to do good on a sabbath. In other words, Jesus was angry at their callousness towards the suffering of the needy.[34]

5. Cursing of the Fig Tree and Cleansing of the Temple (Mark 11:11–25)

> [11] Then he entered Jerusalem and went into the temple; and when he had looked around at everything, as it was already late, he went out to Bethany with the twelve.
> [12] On the following day, when they came from Bethany, he was hungry. [13] Seeing in the distance a fig tree in leaf, he went to see whether perhaps he would find anything on it. When he came to it, he found nothing but leaves, for it was not the season for figs. [14] He said to it, "May no one ever eat fruit from you again." And his disciples heard it.

---

33. I disagree with David P. Nystrom, *James*, NIVAC (Grand Rapids: Zondervan, 1997), 91, that "James is instructing us to be slow to assume the mantle of righteous indignation." Rather, James is dealing with selfish anger, not righteous indignation. Similarly, Lester, *Angry Christian*, 147, concludes that James is alluding to human anger that contributes to alienation rather than reconciliation.

34. Robert H. Gundry, *Mark: A Commentary on His Apology for the Cross* (Grand Rapids: Eerdmans, 1993), 151. David E. Garland, *Mark*, NIVAC (Grand Rapids: Zondervan, 1996), 108, observes that Jesus's anger provoked him to do the only healing miracle that he initiated without prompting (Mark 3:3).

¹⁵ Then they came to Jerusalem. And he entered the temple and began to drive out those who were selling and those who were buying in the temple, and he overturned the tables of the money-changers and the seats of those who sold doves; ¹⁶ and he would not allow anyone to carry anything through the temple. ¹⁷ He was teaching and saying, "Is it not written,

'My house shall be called a house of prayer for all the nations'?
But you have made it a den of robbers.'"

¹⁸ And when the chief priests and the scribes heard it, they kept looking for a way to kill him; for they were afraid of him, because the whole crowd was spellbound by his teaching. ¹⁹ And when evening came, Jesus and his disciples went out of the city.

²⁰ In the morning as they passed by, they saw the fig tree withered away to its roots. ²¹ Then Peter remembered and said to him, "Rabbi, look! The fig tree that you cursed has withered." ²² Jesus answered them, "Have faith in God. ²³ Truly I tell you, if you say to this mountain, 'Be taken up and thrown into the sea,' and if you do not doubt in your heart, but believe that what you say will come to pass, it will be done for you. ²⁴ So I tell you, whatever you ask for in prayer, believe that you have received it, and it will be yours.

²⁵ "Whenever you stand praying, forgive, if you have anything against anyone; so that your Father in heaven may also forgive you your trespasses."

In this account, Jesus took some extreme actions. If Jesus is a model for righteous anger, then we need to understand the following: (1) Why did Jesus curse the fig tree, especially when it was not in season? (2) What made Jesus angry in the temple? (3) Is Jesus teaching about unconditional forgiveness in verse 25?

First, was Jesus simply "hangry" (a slang word for anger caused by hunger)? The usual explanation that softens Jesus's condemnation of the fig tree is that small green figs would sprout during the Passover season, together with the leaves. While not palatable, they are edible, and, apparently, Jesus was hungry enough for such sustenance. However, Mark explains that it was *not* the season for figs (11:13); instead, he twice mentions the "leaves" of the tree, implying that its lushness gave a false impression that it might have some ripening fruit.[35] In the context, Jesus used the fig tree as a symbol for God's people.[36] His point is not so much about bearing fruit at the right time but about people not producing the life that God is looking for, despite their outward (leafy) display of religiosity in the temple.[37]

Second, what caused Jesus to be angry with the people in the temple? Was it their focus on profit-making or their lack of prayer? The merchants were providing a necessary service because only certain kinds of coins were approved for the temple tax, and animals were needed for sacrifices. While some commentators believe that this led to profiteering by the temple authorities, it is best to get our cue from Jesus's citation of the OT in Mark 11:17.

Jesus's pronouncement "My house shall be called a house of prayer for all the nations" is from Isaiah 56:7. The money exchange and the selling of animals could have been conducted outside the temple precincts, but no thought was given to the Gentiles. In contrast, Isaiah 56:1–8 focuses on foreigners coming to the temple. Craig A. Evans points out the parallel with Solomon's prayer in 1 Kings 8:41–43, asking God to hear when Gentiles pray towards his house.[38] This anticipates the new kind of community that Jesus will establish to replace the temple – a community that includes outsiders.[39]

This emphasis on an inclusive worship community leads to Jesus's teaching about prayer and forgiveness in Mark 11:20–25. Tan Kim Huat explains that the temple will no longer be needed for prayer, but requests will be heard by faith. So also, forgiveness will no longer be obtained by sacrifices but by prayers made in a spirit of forgiveness.[40] So, is Jesus teaching about unconditional forgiveness

---

35. R. T. France, *The Gospel of Mark*, NIGTC (Grand Rapids: Eerdmans, 2002), 440; Kim Huat Tan, *The Gospel according to Mark*, ABC (Manila: Asia Theological Association, 2011), 267.

36. France, *Mark*, 441. In Mic 7:1, God laments that he could not find figs *after* the season and goes on to indict Israel for their social ills.

37. Matthew's parallel account in Matt 21 does not mention the season. The same point is made about Jesus looking for righteous lives, but Mark decries the outward ostentatiousness as well.

38. Craig A. Evans, *Mark 8:27 – 16:20*, WBC (Nashville: Thomas Nelson, 2001), 178.

39. Jesus also refers to Jer 7:11, "But you have made it a den of robbers." Jeremiah was asking the temple worshippers, "Will you steal, murder, commit adultery, swear falsely . . . and then come and stand before me in this house . . . ?" (Jer 7:9–10). From Jeremiah's context, Jesus was indicting what people did not just in the temple but also outside it. They did not come to God's house to pray but merely to go through the rituals. France, *Mark*, 446, and Evans, *Mark 8:27 – 16:20*, 175, 182, limit Jesus's judgment to the leaders, not the people. However, this is better supported in Matthew where Jesus's words were addressed to the merchants (Matt 21:12).

40. Tan, *Mark*, 273. Contra France, 448, and Evans, 184, that the saying on forgiveness was added later. In comparison, the parallel account in Matt 21:18–22 does not include the teaching on forgiveness. While Matthew focused only on Jesus's conflict with the temple authorities, Mark is concerned with God's new inclusive community of faith, described in Isa 56:1–7.

in 11:25? Note that Jesus himself said not a word of forgiveness to those he drove out.[41] Instead, the curse of the fig tree shows that the unrighteous will be judged. In fact, Jesus also pronounced curses on other occasions.

6. Jesus's Pronouncements of Woe in the Synoptic Gospels

Jesus uttered thirteen woes in Matthew and fifteen in Luke (Mark has only two). The majority of the situations show that woes were pronounced on recipients who deserved it.[42] There are two questions to consider: (1) Do woes reflect sorrow or anger? (2) How can we reconcile Jesus's judgment with love for enemies?

First, John Day writes that there is a close relationship between "woe" and "curse," although they are not identical. In the OT, such similarities can be seen most clearly in Zechariah 11:17, where a woe is parallel to a curse:[43]

> Oh [woe], my worthless shepherd,
>   who deserts the flock!
> May the sword strike his arm
>   and his right eye!
> Let his arm be completely withered,
>   his right eye utterly blinded!

However, to determine the tone of the woe, much depends on the context. A woe essentially describes a miserable situation, whether the addressees realize it or not.[44] The tone of anger is unmistakable in Jesus's invective against the Pharisees in Matthew 23. He calls them "hypocrites" six times and labels them "child[ren] of hell," "blind guides," "blind fools," "blind men," "blind

---

41. Anthony Bash, *Just Forgiveness: Exploring the Bible, Weighing the Issues* (London: SPCK, 2011), 14.

42. Most of the incidents in Matthew and Luke overlap except for Luke's version of the Beatitudes (Luke 6:24–25). The rest of the incidents involved unresponsive towns (Matt 11:21// Luke 10:13), stumbling blocks (Matt 18:7//Luke 17:1), Pharisees and scribes (Matt 23:13–39// Luke 11:42–52), pregnant and nursing mothers (Mark 13:17//Matt 24:19//Luke 21:23), and the one who betrayed him (Mark 14:21//Matt 25:24//Luke 22:22).

43. John N. Day, *Crying for Justice: What the Psalms Teach Us about Mercy and Vengeance in an Age of Terrorism* (Leicester: Inter-Varsity Press, 2005), 89, n. 166. Elsewhere, there is also similarity in form, content, and context between a woe and a curse: Deut 27:24, "Cursed be anyone who strikes down a neighbour in secret"; and Hab 2:12, "Alas [woe] for you who build a town by bloodshed, and found a city on iniquity!"

44. Nolland, *Matthew*, 467.

Pharisee[s]," "snakes . . . brood of vipers."[45] While these epithets are not used in Luke, he calls them "unmarked graves" (Luke 11:44; Matt 23:27, "whitewashed tombs"), which would be repulsive to Pharisees with their concern for purity. Jesus was furious because the Pharisees were hindering others from entering the kingdom of God (Matt 23:13).

Second, how can we reconcile Jesus's vitriol with the command to love and bless enemies (Matt 5:44)? Some commentators suggest that Jesus was not practising what he preached or that Matthew did not represent Christ rightly.[46] However, immediately after his imprecations, Jesus continues with a lament in Matthew 23:37–39:

> Jerusalem, Jerusalem, the city that kills the prophets and stones those who are sent to it! How often have I desired to gather your children together as a hen gathers her brood under her wings, and you were not willing! See, your house is left to you, desolate. For I tell you, you will not see me again until you say, "Blessed is the one who comes in the name of the Lord."

The address to Jerusalem would include the Pharisees and the scribes, since they were accused of killing prophets sent to them. Jesus laments over his people, like a mother hen over her brood. Thus, his imprecations are warnings out of his love for his people. Nonetheless, love does not exclude judgment.[47]

In summary, the NT texts show that Jesus expressed anger against the Pharisees for doing harm and against the temple worshippers for not bearing fruit. As for human anger, Matthew 5:21–26 and James 1:19–20 warn against anger that is destructive to others. While James implies that the emotion of anger itself is not wrong, we need to examine our motives and actions. Similarly, Ephesians 4:26 warns us not to keep brewing in rage, yet there is the imperative to be angry

---

45. France, *Matthew*, 867, also points out that Jesus's use of "fools" here, in contrast to Matt 5:22 discussed earlier, shows that this is not a thoughtless insult but a considered verdict on the Pharisees' lack of understanding.

46. France, *Matthew*, 867, n. 16; Ulrich Luz, *Matthew 21–28*, Hermeneia (Minneapolis: Fortress, 2005), 138.

47. Hagner, *Matthew 1–13*, 681, points out that commentators disagree whether Matt 23:39 refers to the AD 70 destruction of Jerusalem or to Jesus's parousia (his second coming). It is also unclear whether the acknowledgment of Jesus is said in remorse or gladness, though both are possible. Some Pharisees turned to Jesus; e.g. John's gospel tells us about Nicodemus, the apostle Paul himself was a Pharisee, and there were Pharisees in the early church (Acts 15:5). Hagner, 683, warns us against anti-Semitism because the real enemy is hypocrisy, not the Pharisees or the Jews.

against sin. How are we to work through our anger? I propose that imprecatory psalms show us the way, and we will explore them in later chapters.

Conclusion

Anger is listed as one of the "Seven Deadly Sins" developed by the medieval church. Pastoral care professor Andrew Lester discusses some factors that contributed to the church's view of anger. For instance, classical Greek philosophy prioritized reason over emotion. Early Christian apologists also wanted to demonstrate the difference between their God and the Greco-Roman gods. While the latter were driven by passion, the early church fathers taught that God did not feel anger. Thus, a dualistic view was developed in the monastic period, setting the flesh against the spirit. Emotions like anger were part of the flesh and were to be overcome.[48]

However, Lester points out that some of the church's theologians recognized a place for anger. Augustine of Hippo, though believing that God did not feel anger, wrote that there is no fault with wrath against a wrongdoer.[49] Martin Luther similarly said that anger should be hostile to sin and is a vital motivator: "If I want to write, pray, preach well, then I must be angry. Then my entire blood supply refreshes itself, my mind is made keen, and all temptations depart."[50] John Calvin worried about losing his temper yet paradoxically considered emotions to be part of our unfallen nature and, thus, not sinful.[51] For John Wesley, his idea of "sanctification" meant that Christians would no longer experience anger, yet he wrote, "Anger at sin we allow."[52]

After his survey of the church's teaching, Lester concludes: "We're called to manage anger intelligently, that is, to bring our reason, our will, our values, and our faith into the role of directing this emotion so that it does not become life-destroying, but instead serves its original purpose to be life-enhancing."[53] How is anger life-enhancing? Using neuroscience, Lester explains: "Anger is

---

48. Lester, *Angry Christian*, 117–33.

49. Saint Augustine, *The City of God*, book 9, ch. 5, trans. Marcus Dod (New York: Modern Library, 1993), 285.

50. Martin Luther, *What Luther Says: An Anthology*, Vol. 1, compiled by Ewald M. Plass (St. Louis: Concordia, 1959), entry no. 28, 29.

51. John Calvin, *Commentaries on the Last Four Books of Moses Arranged in the Form of a Harmony* (Grand Rapids: Eerdmans, 1950), 347.

52. John Wesley, "Upon Our Lord's Sermon on the Mount," sermon 22 in *The Works of John Wesley*, Vol. 5 (Grand Rapids: Zondervan, 1958), 264.

53. Lester, *Angry Christian*, 136.

the physical, mental, and emotional arousal pattern that occurs in response to a *perceived threat* to the self, characterised by the desire to attack or defend." A "perceived threat" means people may react differently to the same situation, since they are shaped by their own past experiences.[54]

Alice came to see me because she felt something was wrong with her. She had lost all motivation in her work, felt depressed and lethargic, and experienced a strange "numbness" in her head. As I explored with her about her past, I realized that her physical numbness was a symptom of her emotional repression. Her parents valued academic success to the point of discrimination. Her smart elder sister was lavishly rewarded for doing well – expensive books, shiny new toys, and anything she asked for. In contrast, Alice didn't do well in school, despite her best efforts. For that, she was caned and even made to kneel on the floor. Alice kept her resentment to herself, fearing further punishment if she were to appear insolent.

In her teenage years, Alice became a Christian, which brought her much comfort, but the church's teachings reinforced her belief that all anger was wrong. So, she stuffed her feelings deeper inside until she couldn't feel them any more. But, whenever something unfair happened at work, her rage threatened to erupt, and she subconsciously used all her energy to repress it, leaving her depleted emotionally and physically.

I encouraged her to voice her anger about her childhood experiences to God. Initially, she couldn't bring herself to do it, but she let me pray on her behalf. Step by slow step, she started expressing her feelings to God. I had to help her build an emotional vocabulary from mild annoyance to burning fury. Eventually, her prayers crescendoed from monotonous statements to vehement demands for vindication. When she got in touch with her anger and dealt with it, she eventually recovered her ability to enjoy her life and work.

Does praying about anger include forgiveness? In the following chapters, we will learn what the Bible teaches about forgiveness.

---

54. Lester, 83, 111 (italics original).

2

Is Forgiveness Conditional or Unconditional?

Christians should forgive. Christians should *not* forgive.

The first statement is widely believed, while the second is considered unbiblical. Yet both are true. It took me many years to learn this. Like most pastors, I once experienced a painful conflict in ministry, but I just forgave and moved on. At least, I thought I did. But every time the incident came to mind, I got triggered and teary. Had I not forgiven enough?

One day, early in my seminary teaching career, I was lecturing on the lament and imprecatory psalms in class, trying to convince the students that it was OK to pour out our complaints to God. I explained that complaining in the lament psalms means expressing our hurts and anger, even raising a clenched fist at our enemies as the psalmists did.

As I was speaking, a moment of clarity struck me. This was why the past still haunted me: my hurt was still buried under the veneer of forgiveness. That evening, I found an isolated spot in a nearby park and started yelling out my frustrations to God. I felt a deep sense of relief, knowing that I had cast the problem on God. Healing begins by being honest with God about your struggles, for then he can meet with and restore you.

An author recently wrote that forgiveness is not forgetting the past, overlooking wrongdoing, maintaining harmony at all costs, or a one-sided act to release one's own pain.[1] All these I did so that I could get on with the ministry. I could add one more item to the list of "what forgiveness is not": it is not trying to be a spiritual example by denying one's rage or depression.

---

1. John C. W. Tran, *Authentic Forgiveness: A Biblical Approach* (Carlisle: Langham, 2020), 2.

However, every time I teach the lament and imprecatory psalms, students push back, especially from the NT: "Shouldn't we forgive our enemies?" "Isn't that what Jesus taught us to pray?" "Didn't he forgive his enemies at the cross?" When I'm counselling students and telling them to be emotionally authentic like the psalmists, they still struggle to do it. Eventually, when they are convinced enough to follow the biblical example, they experience the transforming power of God in their lives.

Even if we are convinced that it is acceptable to pour out our hurts and anger to God, should we forgive the wrongdoer unconditionally? There is a long-running philosophical and theological debate on whether forgiveness is dependent on the sinner's repentance. Before diving into the biblical texts in the following chapters, I will briefly summarize the discussion.

The Forgiveness Debate: Conditional or Unconditional?[2]

The traditional belief is that forgiveness is unconditional – that is, we should forgive regardless of whether the offender repents because that is what God wants us to do. However, I believe that the more biblical and justifiable position is that forgiveness is conditional – that is, it is dependent on repentance. Where there is no repentance, one is to act with love. The difference between forgiveness and love will be clarified in chapter 5.

We begin the debate with R. C. Moberly, who in *Atonement and Personality* (1901) stated that true forgiveness does not condone wrong. It is, thus, conditional on the "forgivableness" or penitence of the wrongdoer.[3] However, in *The Christian Experience of Forgiveness* (1927), H. R. Mackintosh argued that forgiveness comes from the unconditional grace of God and is what causes the forgiven person to change.[4]

In *The Forgiveness of Sins* (1937), Basil Redlich tried to integrate the need for repentance with grace by arguing that the NT requires the offended person to be active in wooing the offender back. He calls this a spirit of

2. This debate is adapted from Nigel Biggar, "Forgiveness in the Twentieth Century," in *Forgiveness and Truth: Exploration in Contemporary Theology*, eds. Alistair McFadyen and Marcel Sarot (Edinburgh: T&T Clark, 2001), 181–217; Kit Barker, *Imprecation as Divine Discourse: Speech Act Theory, Dual Authorship, and Theological Interpretation* (Winona Lake: Eisenbrauns, 2016), 137–45; and Tran, *Authentic Forgiveness*, 29–54.

3. R. C. Moberly, *Atonement and Personality* (1901; repr., London: Murray, 1907), 52–53, 56, 61.

4. H. R. Mackintosh, *The Christian Experience of Forgiveness* (London: Harper & Brothers, 1927), 131, 181, 265, 255.

"forgivingness."[5] However, this would make it hard for some victims. Can one expect a physically, emotionally, or sexually abused victim to woo her oppressor back? It would be a sadistic burden or reinforce an unhealthy co-dependent relationship. Richard Swinburne recognized this problem in *Responsibility and Atonement* (1989), pointing out that unconditional forgiveness in the case of serious injury would trivialize the wrong done.[6]

Baptist theologian Paul Fiddes took the unconditional view in *Past Event and Present Salvation* (1989), contending that Jesus welcomed sinners without waiting for them to repent.[7] Similarly, L. Gregory Jones, in *Embodying Forgiveness* (1995), based forgiveness on the Trinity because, in the incarnation, God did not wait for the prodigal children's return but undertook the journey into the far country to search for them. Repentance is the response to this act of grace. In fact, Jones's insistence on the pre-eminence of grace and forgiveness led him to harbour hopes for universal redemption.[8]

It is worth mentioning a moral philosopher, Joram Graf Haber, who, in *Forgiveness* (1991), made the case that forgiveness is a virtue only if given for a moral reason, differentiating it from therapeutic forgetting. That means forgiveness should be exercised only when there is repentance and not just for the sake of making the victim feel better.[9]

Miroslav Volf offered a more nuanced view in *Exclusion and Embrace* (1996). He wrote that reconciliation begins with identifying with one's oppressor in our human sinfulness, which grows into "the will to embrace," that is, the will to be reconciled with the enemy. However, "the embrace itself" or complete reconciliation can happen only when there is repentance, which he defined as truth-telling and doing justice. While theologically valid, it is emotionally difficult for a victim to be willing to embrace a violent offender. Thus, Volf counsels sufferers to place their hatred before God, who loves and does justice. He is also realistic in acknowledging that some ruptures in

---

5. Basil Redlich, *The Forgiveness of Sins* (Edinburgh: T&T Clark, 1937), 100–101, 104–5, 111.

6. Richard Swinburne, *Responsibility and Atonement* (Oxford: Oxford University Press, 1989), 85–86.

7. Paul Fiddes, *Past Event and Present Salvation: The Christian Idea of Atonement* (Louisville: Westminster John Knox, 1989), 173–77. In the next chapter, I will show that Jesus's welcome of sinners presumes their faith and repentance.

8. L. Gregory Jones, *Embodying Forgiveness: A Theological Analysis* (Grand Rapids: Eerdmans, 1995), 118–19, 144, 146, 152–55, 253.

9. Joram Graf Haber, *Forgiveness* (Savage: Rowman & Littlefield, 1991), 90–110.

relationships cannot be fully repaired, so sometimes, forgiveness has to be in the form of people going their separate ways in peace.[10]

In recent decades, much has been written about forgiveness from a psychological dimension, beginning with Lewis Smedes's *Forgive and Forget: Healing the Hurts We Don't Deserve* (1984), followed by a collection of more scientific essays edited by Everett Worthington in *Dimensions of Forgiveness: Psychological Research and Theological Perspective* (1998). These writings advise a victim to forgive in order to be healed of negative emotions, regardless of whether the wrongdoer repents. A distinction is made between forgiveness and reconciliation – the former is *intra*personal and unconditional, while the latter is *inter*personal and dependent on the offender's response.[11]

The problem with such "therapeutic" forgiveness, as Nigel Biggar pointed out, is that it completely neglects the dimensions of culpability and justice.[12] The offender is not disciplined, the wrong is not made right, and restoration of the relationship can be side-stepped.[13] Additionally, Nicholas Wolterstorff, in *Justice in Love* (2011), wrote that such an approach devalues morality and personhood. It does not treat "the deed or its doer with the moral seriousness required for forgiveness; it is to downplay rather than to forgive. 'I suppose he did wrong me; but it's not worth making anything of it.'"[14] Such thinking

---

10. Miroslav Volf, *Exclusion and Embrace: A Theological Exploration of Identity, Otherness, and Reconciliation* (Nashville: Abingdon, 1996), 29, 81, 224, 124–26. In a subsequent book, *Free of Charge: Giving and Forgiving in a Culture Stripped of Grace; The Archbishop's Official 2006 Lent Book* (Grand Rapids: Zondervan, 2005), Miroslav Volf elevated forgiveness to an unconditional act: "forgivers will keep forgiving, whether the offenders repent or not." However, without repentance, "the offenders will remain unforgiven, in that they are untouched by that forgiveness" (183). Kit Barker, in *Imprecation as Divine Discourse*, 143–44, argued that Volf is contradictory here: the victim may keep forgiving, but such forgiveness has no effect without repentance. It would be more consistent to say that one should be willing to forgive (like the will to embrace), rather than that one actually forgives.

11. Lewis B. Smedes, *Forgive and Forget: Healing the Hurts We Don't Deserve* (San Francisco: Harper & Row, 1984); Everett L. Worthington, ed., *Dimensions of Forgiveness: Psychological Research and Theological Perspectives* (Philadelphia: Templeton Foundation Press, 1998).

12. Biggar, "Forgiveness," 214.

13. In a subsequent book, *A Just Forgiveness: Responsible Healing without Excusing Injustice* (Downers Grove: InterVarsity Press, 2009), Everett L. Worthington tried to hold both unconditional forgiveness and repentance together. Nonetheless, his guidelines for forgiveness were still an individualistic psychological exercise in freeing oneself: "Have you ever harmed or offended a friend, parent or partner who later forgave you? . . . As you remember how you felt when you were forgiven – free, light or unburdened – you might be more willing to give a selfless gift of forgiveness to the one who hurt you" (104).

14. Nicholas Wolterstorff, *Justice in Love*, Emory University Studies in Law and Religion (Grand Rapids: Eerdmans, 2011), 173, cited in Barker, *Imprecation as Divine Discourse*, 140.

devalues the offended person because he or she has to disregard personal grievances and feelings.

Not every Christian counsellor holds the same view as Smedes and Worthington. David W. Augsburger, in *Helping People Forgive* (1996), wrote that forgiveness is "the mutual recognition that repentance is genuine (repentance by one or both parties) and right relationships have been restored or achieved."[15] Augsburger has a holistic concept of forgiveness but is perhaps too idealistic in expecting reconciliation. Though that is the right goal, Volf has pointed out that we might have to forgive without full reconciliation because we live in a fallen world.

Where Augsburger's view strongly resonates with me is in his distinction between love and forgiveness: "Love may be unconditional, forgiveness is not. . . . Is it appropriate to speak of unconditional forgiveness, or should we more correctly refer to this as acceptance or love?"[16] In the following four chapters, I will show that the Bible never tells us to forgive our enemies unconditionally, but it does tell us to love them.

The difference between love and forgiveness is well illustrated by Victor Hugo's depiction of kind-hearted Bishop Myriel in his novel *Les Misérables*. The bishop welcomed Jean Valjean, a homeless criminal, to stay with him, but Valjean made away with the bishop's silverware in the middle of the night. The police found the thief and dragged him back, but the clergyman unexpectedly said that the items were a gift and even claimed that Valjean had forgotten to take a pair of silver candlesticks as well. The police had no choice but to let the thief go. Shaken by this act of undeserved grace, Valjean resolved to turn his life around.

I used to be bothered that the bishop seemed to forgive without requiring repentance. Now I recognize that he was not imparting forgiveness but, rather, a love that sought the criminal's redemption and change. In the musical, Bishop Myriel sings:

> But remember this, my brother,
> See in this some higher plan.
> You must use this precious silver
> To become an honest man.
> By the witness of the martyrs,
> By the Passion and the Blood,

---

15. David W. Augsburger, *Helping People Forgive* (Louisville: Westminster John Knox, 1996), 14–16.

16. Augsburger, *Helping People Forgive*, 14.

God has raised you out of darkness;
I have bought your soul for God!

The bishop did not mention forgiveness but urged repentance, telling Valjean that he was accountable to God. Valjean responded with the following soliloquy expressing remorse and determination to change, which is played out in the rest of the story:

My life he claims for God above.
Can such things be? . . .
. . . He offers me my freedom.
I feel my shame inside me like a knife. . . .
What spirit comes to move my life?
Is there another way to go? . . .
Jean Valjean is nothing now!
Another story must begin![17]

Definitions of Repentance and Forgiveness

Since forgiveness depends on repentance, we need to understand what repentance is. Augsburger writes that in the Christian tradition, it has three dimensions: remorse, restitution, and renewal. "First, a genuine sorrow is necessary; second, an attempt to restore what was destroyed as far as possible; third, a change in life direction."[18]

1. Remorse. First John 1:9 and James 5:16 tell us that to be forgiven, one has to confess, which is to admit the wrong done. Though we cannot assess the offender's sincerity, there is at least some expression of remorse or regret.

2. Restitution. The OT laws require compensation for property damage (Exod 22:1–15; Lev 6:1–7). Restitution ranges from repaying the principal to doubling the amount depending on the situation. In other words, repentance includes the willingness to accept loss or some form of punishment.

3. Renewal. A change of behaviour is required: "Bear fruit worthy of repentance" (Matt 3:8; Luke 3:8). The Greek word for repentance, *metanoia*, means "change of mind." Since forgiveness is not about overlooking but righting a wrong, the offender must show that he or she is making an effort to do right. Only then can both parties work towards a restoration of the relationship.

---

17. Alain Albert Boublil, Claude Michel Schonberg, Herbet Kretzmer, and Jean Marc Natel, "The Bishop" and "Valjean's Soliloquy," in *Les Misérables: A Musical* (London: Alain Boublil Music; exclusively distributed by H. Leonard, 1998).

18. Augsburger, *Helping People Forgive*, 16.

Forgiveness mirrors the above three elements of repentance in recognizing the wrong, releasing debt, and restoring relationships.[19]

1. Recognition of Wrong. Rather than being passive-aggressive, Matthew 18:15 exhorts the offended person to go and point out the other party's fault, implying that there is a moral issue involved. It may turn out that there was simply a misunderstanding, in which case clarification is all that is required. Often, a conflict is due to personality differences; what is needed then are mutual adjustments or mediation.

2. Release from Debt. In Matthew 6:12, Jesus taught his disciples to pray, "And forgive us our debts, as we also have forgiven our debtors." The Greek word for forgiveness is *aphiēmi*, used in relation to forgiving a debt. The Hebrew word usually used for forgiveness is *nasa*, which means to "lift, carry," that is, to take away the burden of guilt. Forgiveness, then, is to remove the burden of what is owed, as demonstrated in the parable of the unforgiving servant in Matthew 18:23–35. The astronomical amount owed by the servant was impossible for him to repay, yet the king completely released him from it. Kit Barker puts it well that forgiveness involves cancelling a debt that outweighs complete restitution.[20] Even if compensation is made, it cannot restore the one harmed to his or her original condition: a substitute item is not the original, an injury leaves scars, and hurt cannot be un-experienced. Thus, conditional forgiveness is still an exercise of grace. It brings psychological healing as a side effect because the creditor can let go of keeping accounts mentally and emotionally.

3. Restoration of Relationship. In Jesus's parable of the prodigal son, the father joyfully welcomed and reinstated his repentant son. However, as pointed out by Volf, reconciliation may take time in a broken world. Even Paul and Barnabas had such a sharp disagreement over Mark that they parted company (Acts 15:39). However, at the end of Paul's ministry, he asked for Mark, "for he is useful in my ministry" (2 Tim 4:11). In their case, it seems to have been a clash of opinions or personalities rather than a moral conflict. Nonetheless, whatever the cause, reconciliation takes time because people are in the process of learning and growing. Even where repentance and forgiveness have been

---

19. Barker, *Imprecation as Divine Discourse*, 138, also presents three aspects: (1) count the actions of another as wrongdoing; (2) recognize that the wrongdoer's transgression has produced a debt that outweighs complete restitution; (3) accept the wrongdoer's apology, which means to treat the wrongdoer as though he or she owes you nothing more in this regard. I combine his second and third points and add the last step of working towards reconciliation.

20. Barker, 138.

extended, the trauma may be so deep that time and space are needed for healing. In the meantime, we can still bless the one who hurt us.

Conclusion

In sum, both statements are true: Christians should forgive, and Christians should *not* forgive. It depends on whether the offender repents for the wrong done. We will see what the NT and OT teach about forgiveness and repentance in the following two chapters. We begin with the NT because most people assume it mandates unconditional forgiveness.

3

What Is Forgiveness in the New Testament?

"Don't tell me to forgive my husband! I wish he would go to hell!"

When I met Lindy, she was going through a bitter divorce. She was so frightened of her abusive husband that she would lock herself in the bathroom whenever he got into a violent rage. Finally, she had enough. Lindy used to go to church, so when I paid her a pastoral visit she assumed that I would tell her to forgive her husband and wanted to let me know that she would have none of it. I told Lindy that she could tell God how angry she was.

"Then can I tell God I want him to go to hell?" she pressed.

"You can tell God whatever you want, as long as you let God be the judge," I replied. "Who is the one who can punish him better – you or God?"

"All right, it's God. But God will just forgive him in the end, won't he?" she protested.

I explained that God is a God of justice and will not let the guilty go scot-free. Eventually, she let me pray with her, which was the first step in her journey towards healing.

Most Christians assume that the Bible requires us to forgive, no matter how grievous the sin. In the first part of this chapter, we will look at five NT texts that seem to teach that forgiveness is unconditional:

- The Lord's Prayer
- The healing of the paralytic
- The woman caught in adultery
- Jesus's crucifixion
- Paul's exhortations to forgive one another

I will show that with proper exegesis, these texts do *not* support unconditional forgiveness. In the second part of the chapter, we will look at another five texts that show the necessity of repentance:

- Luke's parables of the lost
- The Pharisee and the tax collector
- Zacchaeus
- Two texts from the epistles about forgiveness

Forgiveness Is Not Conditional on Repentance?
1. The Lord's Prayer (Matt 6:12, 14–15)

[12] And forgive us our debts, as we also have forgiven our debtors. . . .[1]

[14] For if you forgive others their trespasses, your heavenly Father will also forgive you; [15] but if you do not forgive others, neither will your Father forgive your trespasses.

The Lord's Prayer seems to make forgiveness an absolute duty, but Jesus's parable in Matthew 18:23–35 about the unforgiving servant points to God's forgiveness as the basis and model for human forgiveness.[2] So, if we are to forgive like God, we need to see how God forgives in Matthew 18:23–35 and its parallel in Luke 17:3–4. It will be seen that repentance *is* a condition for forgiveness.

We begin with Peter's question about forgiveness in Matthew 18:21–22, which introduces the parable about the unforgiving servant: "Then Peter came and said to him, 'Lord, if another member of the church sins against me, how often should I forgive? As many as seven times?' Jesus said to him, 'Not seven times, but, I tell you, seventy-seven times.'"

Since seven represents perfection in the biblical context, seventy-seven times is a hyperbole, meaning that there is no limit to forgiveness,[3] but does it mean that one should forgive irrespective of the offender's attitude? There are

---

1. Matthew uses "we have forgiven," a Greek aorist, to show that forgiving others must be done before asking God for forgiveness. This is, however, a day-by-day practice, given that the Lord's Prayer is to be prayed on a daily basis. The Lucan parallel supports this reading, as Luke 11:4 uses the Greek present tense "we forgive," indicating an ongoing practice of forgiveness of others. John Nolland, *Luke 9:21 – 18:35*, WBC (Dallas: Word, 1993), 618, says: "The daily flow of forgiveness from God would be impeded if there were not a corresponding practice of forgiveness at the human level."

2. France, *Matthew*, 252; Hagner, *Matthew 1–13*, 152.

3. France, 705. For one thing, creation was completed on the seventh day (Gen 2:2).

three reasons why repentance is assumed, based on (1) the following parable in Matthew 18:23–35, (2) the preceding teaching on church discipline in Matthew 18:15–20, and (3) the parallel text in Luke 17:3–4.

First, in the subsequent parable, a king forgives a servant who owed him ten thousand talents, an unimaginable amount of money, as one talent was what a labourer might hope to earn in half a lifetime.[4] When the king demanded to be paid or else he would sell off the servant and his family, "the slave fell on his knees before him, saying, 'Have patience with me, and I will pay you everything'" (18:26). Then, out of compassion, the king forgave him the debt. The servant's plea to make things right, even though seemingly impossible, portrayed his repentance.

However, it proved to be false repentance because the servant showed no change of behaviour but continued in his greedy ways. He violently demanded that his fellow servant pay him back a hundred denarii (about three or four months' wages).[5] Despite the second servant begging for patience in words similar to his own, the first servant threw him into prison. When this was reported to the king, the ruler got angry and handed the ungrateful servant over to be tortured in jail. Jesus ended his parable by saying, "So my heavenly Father will also do to every one of you, if you do not forgive your brother or sister from your heart" (18:35).

The moral of the parable is to forgive others because God has forgiven us infinitely more for our debt to him. The servant's desperate supplication was enough to gain forgiveness, but genuine repentance must be demonstrated by acting like the divine forgiver. When the servant showed no remorse, the royal pardon was rescinded and the punishment executed. If we follow God's example, then we are to forgive those who sincerely repent, meaning that forgiveness is conditional.

Second, Jesus was teaching about church discipline in Matthew 18:15–20, and it was this which provoked Peter's question about how many times one needs to forgive.

> [15] If another member of the church sins [against you],[6] go and point out the fault when the two of you are alone. If the member

---

4. France, 706.

5. France, 707.

6. There is uncertainty whether "against you" is a late addition in the light of Peter's question in 18:21 about someone who sins "against me." The absence of the phrase would imply that a member's sin needs to be dealt with whether one is the offended party or not. In any case, the instructions would certainly be relevant to the offended person (France, 689; Hagner, *Matthew 1–13*, 529).

> listens to you, you have regained that one. [16] But if you are not
> listened to, take one or two others along with you, so that every
> word may be confirmed by the evidence of two or three witnesses.
> [17] If the member refuses to listen to them, tell it to the church; and
> if the offender refuses to listen even to the church, let such a one
> be to you as a Gentile and a tax-collector.

The offended party is not told to forgive but to "go and point out the fault when the two of you are alone." After all, it may only be a misunderstanding that needs clarification rather than forgiveness. However, if the person is at fault and refuses to listen, two or three others must be brought along as witnesses (18:16). If the accused listens, implying that he or she is willing to correct the fault, the relationship is restored.[7]

If the person refuses to listen, then "let such a one be to you as a Gentile and a tax-collector" (18:17), an idiomatic Jewish expression meaning to suspend fellowship with the offender.[8] In other words, without repentance, there is no reconciliation. Thus, when Peter followed up with his question about forgiveness, he should be understood as asking, "If another member of the church sins against me, how often should I forgive *when he or she repents*?" Jesus's answer should then be understood as, "As often as the person genuinely repents."

The third consideration is that the Lucan parallel confirms this understanding of what Jesus meant in Matthew 18: "Be on your guard! If another disciple sins, you must rebuke the offender, and if there is *repentance*, you must forgive. And if the same person sins against you seven[9] times a day, and *turns back* to you seven times and says, 'I *repent*,' you must forgive" (Luke 17:3–4).

Like Matthew, Luke requires one not merely to forgive or ignore an offender but to rebuke him or her. He echoes the OT teaching in Leviticus 19:17: "You shall not hate in your heart anyone of your kin; you shall reprove your neighbour, or you will incur guilt yourself."[10] Unlike Matthew, Luke does not have Jesus's teaching on church discipline and the parable of the

7. Hagner, 531; Blomberg, *Matthew*, 282.

8. France, *Matthew*, 694.

9. Robert H. Stein, *Luke*, NAC (Nashville: Broadman & Holman, 1992), 430. Like seventy-seven, the number seven is symbolic of completeness, meaning that one should always forgive.

10. James R. Edwards, *The Gospel according to Luke*, PNTC (Grand Rapids: Eerdmans, 2015), 477.

unforgiving servant in his context, so he makes the relation between forgiveness and repentance explicit in this text.

Anthony Bash suggests that Luke consistently emphasizes that repentance must precede forgiveness to show his Gentile readers that Christianity was not a threat to good order in society. If Christians were to forgive unrepentant sinners without doing justice, the gospel would result in lawlessness and civil disorder.[11] Thus, the larger context of Matthew's and Luke's Gospels show us that human and divine forgiveness require repentance.

2. The Healing of the Paralytic (Mark 2:5//Matt 9:2//Luke 5:20)

> When Jesus saw their faith, he said to the paralytic, "Son, your sins are forgiven." (Mark 2:5)

The basis for forgiveness here is simply "faith." Does this include repentance? Donald E. Gowan argues that since the paralytic did not ask for forgiveness, Jesus did not require repentance.[12] However, there are two aspects to consider: (1) Jesus's teaching around this healing story, and (2) the meaning of "faith."

First, the story began with Jesus "speaking the word" to the people (Mark 2:2). A summary of what Jesus said can be found in the preceding chapter: "The time is fulfilled, and the kingdom of God has come near; *repent*, and believe in the good news" (Mark 1:15). "Believe" (*pisteuō*) and "faith" (*pistis*) in Greek come from the same root. A series of healings and deliverances then happened in quick succession.

The same emphasis is found in the other Synoptic Gospels. In Matthew, Jesus launched his ministry with the proclamation, "*Repent*, for the kingdom of heaven has come near" (Matt 4:17). This was followed by the Sermon on the Mount and a series of miracles, including the paralytic's healing in Matthew 9:2. In Luke, the story of the paralytic is followed by Jesus's message of repentance in the pericope of Levi's banquet. There, the Pharisees criticized Jesus for fraternizing with tax collectors and sinners, to which he replied, "I have come to call not the righteous but sinners to *repentance*" (Luke 5:32). Thus, Jesus's

---

11. Bash, *Just Forgiveness*, 98.

12. Donald E. Gowan, *The Bible on Forgiveness* (Eugene: Pickwick, 2010), 118–19. Gowan also discusses the pericope of the sinful woman who washed Jesus's feet in Luke 7:36–50. He notes that Jesus similarly pronounced forgiveness and salvation through faith without a need for repentance. However, the woman had already experienced forgiveness prior to this encounter. Since the point of the story is the woman's response of gratitude, the account is silent about her repentance, and we can make no conclusion from this silence.

healing of the paralytic would have assumed the man's repentance.[13] How do we see this attitude demonstrated?

We come to the second point of what faith is in the context of this story. Jesus saw "their" faith, meaning that of the paralytic and his four friends. It was acted out by carrying their friend to Jesus, digging through the roof, and letting the man down into the room before Jesus. Mark had already made it clear in 1:15 that faith presupposed repentance. In Greek, to repent is *metanoeō*, which means to change one's mind, and faith would then direct one towards Christ.[14] Faith turned the sick man and his friends towards Christ, showing that they had turned away from their previous (un)beliefs.

We will now take a closer look at two texts where neither repentance nor faith was mentioned before Jesus announced forgiveness.

3. The Woman Caught in Adultery (John 7:53–8:11)

> [7:53] Then each of them went home, [8:1] while Jesus went to the Mount of Olives. [2] Early in the morning he came again to the temple. All the people came to him and he sat down and began to teach them. [3] The scribes and the Pharisees brought a woman who had been caught in adultery; and making her stand before all of them, [4] they said to him, "Teacher, this woman was caught in the very act of committing adultery. [5] Now in the law Moses commanded us to stone such women. Now what do you say?" [6] They said this to test him, so that they might have some charge to bring against him. Jesus bent down and wrote with his finger on the ground. [7] When they kept on questioning him, he straightened up and said to them, "Let anyone among you who is without sin be the first to throw a stone at her." [8] And once again he bent down and

---

13. Barker, *Imprecation as Divine Discourse*, 146, n. 55, reads Luke 5:32 in the light of Luke 17:3–4 where forgiveness is dependent on repentance. After all, Jesus knew the thoughts of those present (5:22).

14. John Nolland, *Luke 1 – 9:20*, WBC (Dallas: Word, 1989), 235, remarks that faith is "the conviction that God's help is to be found with Jesus and [to] gratefully receive God's action through him." Robert A. Guelich, *Mark 1 – 8:26*, WBC (Dallas: Word, 1989), 85, similarly comments on the Marcan version that "faith involves actions that transcend human obstacles and limitations and cross social boundaries" to receive Jesus's help. E. P. Sanders, *The Historical Figure of Jesus* (London: Penguin, 1993), 125–26, explains that Jesus offered entry into his kingdom to any who followed him, even "though they had not technically 'repented,' and though they had not become righteous in the way required by the law." Moberly, *Atonement and Personality*, 64, writes that "God's love eagerly meets the first glimmer of regret with a loving embrace."

wrote on the ground. [9] When they heard it, they went away, one by one, beginning with the elders; and Jesus was left alone with the woman standing before him. [10] Jesus straightened up and said to her, "Woman, where are they? Has no one condemned you?" [11] She said, "No one, sir." And Jesus said, "Neither do I condemn you. Go your way, and from now on do not sin again."[15]

Jesus's challenge that the one without fault should cast the first stone forces the accusers to examine themselves in the light of the Mosaic law. The OT laws required both the man and the woman caught in the act of adultery to be put to death (Lev 20:10; Deut 22:22–24). Furthermore, the law states that the witnesses to the offence should be the first to throw the stones but warns that those who give malicious and false testimonies should suffer the same punishment as the accused (Deut 17:7; 19:16–18). The Pharisees' behaviour was suspicious because they brought only the female and not the male culprit. When the faultfinders slunk away, it was an admission that none had been actual witnesses.

Thus, when Jesus said to the woman, "Neither do I condemn you," he was not pronouncing forgiveness but simply saying that she did not warrant the death penalty in a public trial. In legal terms, this can be compared to a discharge not amounting to an acquittal. However, we know she was guilty because Jesus told her not to sin again. In other words, Jesus was giving a warning and an opportunity for the adulteress to repent.[16] The placement of this story in John's gospel, between Jesus's claims that he is the river and the light of life (John 7:38; 8:12), also clues us in to its interpretation. Jesus came to offer life in place of death, but sinners need to respond in repentance.

---

15. Most scholars agree that this account was not a part of the original gospel. It does not appear in early Greek manuscripts and is found in the standard Greek text only from AD 900. Others accept it as an early independent story that found its way into John's gospel.

Some scholars argue that Jesus was only commuting the death penalty for adultery. They explain that the Pharisees were trying to trap Jesus by making him choose between the OT law of adultery, which required the death penalty (Lev 20:10; Deut 22:22–24), and the Roman law which did not allow Jewish people to carry out the death sentence (John 18:31). However, J. Ramsey Michaels, *The Gospel of John*, NICNT (Grand Rapids: Eerdmans, 2010), 496, disagrees because Pilate allowed the Jews to execute Jesus according to their law (John 18:31; 19:6). Furthermore, the OT death penalty for adultery could be commuted by compensation (Num 35:31), and the husband might merely divorce his wife (Deut 24:1).

16. So also Leon Morris, *The Gospel according to John*, rev. ed., NICNT (Grand Rapids: Eerdmans, 1995), 786.

4. Jesus at the Cross (Luke 23:34)

> Then Jesus said, "Father, forgive them; for they do not know what they are doing."[17]

This text is often cited as a basis for unconditional forgiveness.[18] However, it should be noted that Jesus is talking about ignorant rather than intentional sins. The sin of ignorance and its purification is found in Leviticus 4: "The LORD spoke to Moses, saying, Speak to the people of Israel, saying: When anyone sins unintentionally in any of the LORD's commandments about things not to be done, and does any one of them . . ." (Lev 4:1–2).

Jacob Milgrom explains that inadvertent wrongdoing may result from two causes: "Negligence or ignorance. Either the offender knows the law but involuntarily violates it or he acts knowingly but is unaware he did wrong." When the offender realizes he or she has broken a commandment, the offender is to bring a guilt offering to God (Lev 4:13–14, 22–23, 27–28). Milgrom equates such guilt with sorrow but notes that no confession of wrongful intention is required.[19]

Bash and Barker also observe that Jesus did not extend forgiveness personally but asked God the Father to do so.[20] The people did not deliberately sin against Jesus, since they were ignorant of Jesus's true identity.[21] However,

---

17. The originality of this prayer is disputed. See Darrell L. Bock, *Luke 9:51 – 24:53*, BECNT (Grand Rapids: Baker, 1996), 1868. One basis for its inclusion is Stephen's parallel prayer in Acts 7:60. In any case, I discuss this text because it is often held up as an example of unconditional forgiveness.

18. Gowan, *Bible on Forgiveness*, 132, qualifies this by saying, "Forgiveness may begin entirely by the initiative of the injured party, but it can never achieve what is intended unless it can be accepted by the guilty one."

19. Jacob Milgrom, *Leviticus 1–16*, AB (New York: Doubleday, 1991), 228, 254, 301. Among other texts, Milgrom cites 1 Sam 14:32–34 as an example of an inadvertent sin. Because of an enforced fast, Saul's troops were so hungry that they killed livestock and ate meat with the blood. Saul hastened to correct his men and told them not to sin against the Lord. He then built an altar, but no confession was recorded.

20. Barker, *Imprecation as Divine Discourse*, 146; Bash, *Just Forgiveness*, 14; Anthony Bash, "Difficult Texts: Luke 23.34 and Acts 7.60 – Forgiving the Unrepentant?," *Theology* 119, no. 4 (2016): 277.

21. The soldiers obviously thought they were merely putting to death a rebel who claimed to be the king of the Jews. The bystanders simply followed their leaders in demanding Jesus's death (Luke 23:18), and the leaders could not believe that he was the Messiah and Son of God, especially when he did not save himself (Luke 22:66–71; 23:35). Gowan, *Bible and Forgiveness*, 129, adds that the leaders also had a political concern, for in the words of the high priest Caiaphas, "it is better for you to have one man die for the people than to have the whole nation destroyed" (John 11:50).

as we can see from the OT's provision for the guilt offering, people need to realize and correct their mistakes.

Luke deals with this motif of ignorance in the book of Acts.[22] The closest example is in Acts 7:60, when Stephen was being stoned to death. Like Jesus he prayed, "Lord, do not hold this sin against them." Paul, who was present at Stephen's martyrdom (Acts 7:58), later testified that he did not know what he was doing. He said in 1 Timothy 1:13, "I was formerly a blasphemer, a persecutor, and a man of violence. But I received mercy because I had acted ignorantly in unbelief." Paul also preached about God's mercy for lack of knowledge. In Acts 17:30–31, he addressed the Athenians, saying that "while God has overlooked the times of human ignorance, now he commands all people everywhere to repent."

Therefore, Jesus's pardon at the cross is not a precedent for unconditional forgiveness. Instead, it shows that we should be gracious to offenders for their lack of knowledge or ability, and seek to help them realize and rectify their mistakes.

5. Forgive One Another (Eph 4:32//Col 3:13)

[31] Put away from you all bitterness and wrath and anger and wrangling and slander, together with all malice, [32] and be kind to one another, tender-hearted, forgiving [*charizomai*] one another, as God in Christ has forgiven [*charizomai*] you. (Eph 4:31–32)

[12] As God's chosen ones, holy and beloved, clothe yourselves with compassion, kindness, humility, meekness, and patience. [13] Bear with one another and, if anyone has a complaint against another, forgive [*charizomai*] each other; just as the Lord has forgiven [*charizomai*] you, so you also must forgive. (Col 3:12–13)

These seem like unconditional commands to forgive. However, we need to consider two things: (1) the Greek root translated as "forgive" in the above two verses, *charizomai*, which is literally "be gracious to"; and (2) the context of these verses.

First, *charizomai* includes forgiveness (usually *aphiēmi*), but it can have a broader meaning of "showing favor, kindness, pleasantness." Hoehner observes that it occurs twenty-three times in the NT, sixteen times in Paul's

---

22. Joel B. Green, *The Gospel of Luke*, NICNT (Grand Rapids: Eerdmans, 1997), 820, n. 29, lists Acts 3:17; 13:27; 14:16; 17:30; 26:9.

writings, and twice in Ephesians. Paul used the word for various situations, such as God giving his Son (Rom 8:32), the gifts of the Spirit (1 Cor 2:12), the Abrahamic inheritance (Gal 3:18), the privilege to suffer for Christ (Phil 1:29), and forgiving our trespasses (Col 2:13). These examples show that *charizomai* means forgiveness when the context refers to sin, as in Colossians 2:13. Therefore, Hoehner astutely argues that "being gracious to one another" is better suited in the above-cited verses because "graciousness is the antithesis of bitterness, anger, wrath, shouting and abusive speech."[23]

Second, the context of Ephesians 4–5 and Colossians 3 calls Christians to put away the old life of sin and put on the new life of Christ. Thus, even if *charizomai* includes forgiveness, it is not an unconditional pardon that forgoes repentance and allows for the continuation of sin. Ephesians 5 warns of God's wrath on the disobedient and commands the church to expose the works of darkness (5:6, 11). Similarly, in Colossians, the church is to teach and admonish one another (Col 3:16).

After these teachings, Paul continues with the household codes, and Colossians 3:22–4:1 instructs slaves what to do when mistreated.

> Slaves, obey your earthly masters in everything, not only while being watched and in order to please them, but wholeheartedly, fearing the Lord. Whatever your task, put yourselves into it, as done for the Lord and not for your masters, since you know that from the Lord you will receive the inheritance as your reward; you serve the Lord Christ. For the wrongdoer will be paid back for whatever wrong has been done, and there is no partiality. Masters, treat your slaves justly and fairly, for you know that you also have a Master in heaven.

When the master has done wrong, the slave is instructed not to forgive but to entrust judgment to God and continue working for the Lord. Thus in the context of the chapter, *charizomai* in Colossians 3:13 does not mean unconditional forgiveness but is better understood as "be gracious to."

We will now turn to five texts that make repentance explicitly necessary for forgiveness.

---

23. Hoehner, *Ephesians*, 639–40.

Forgiveness *Is* Conditional on Repentance
1. Luke's Parables of the Lost (Luke 15)

Luke's first two parables about the lost sheep and the lost coin end with similar sayings:

> [7] Just so, I tell you, there will be more joy in heaven over one sinner who *repents* than over ninety-nine righteous people who need no repentance. . . .
>
> [10] Just so, I tell you, there is joy in the presence of the angels of God over one sinner who *repents.*

Clearly, salvation is dependent on repentance. Jesus then urged the Pharisees to participate with God in welcoming the lost who returned by repentance. Bruce D. Chilton writes, "Repentance is a necessary and inescapable aspect of entering the Kingdom; it is implicit within much of Jesus' discourse, and need not be named to be operative."[24]

The third parable, of the prodigal son, also demonstrates the act of repentance.

> [17] But when he came to himself he said, "How many of my father's hired hands have bread enough and to spare, but here I am dying of hunger! [18] I will get up and go to my father, and I will say to him, 'Father, I have sinned against heaven and before you; [19] I am no longer worthy to be called your son; treat me like one of your hired hands.'" [20] So he set off and went to his father. But while he was still far off, his father saw him and was filled with compassion; he ran and put his arms around him and kissed him. [21] Then the son said to him, "Father, I have sinned against heaven and before you; I am no longer worthy to be called your son." [22] But the father said to his slaves, "Quickly, bring out a robe – the best one – and put it on him; put a ring on his finger and sandals on his feet. [23] And get the fatted calf and kill it, and let us eat and celebrate; [24] for this son of mine was dead and is alive again; he was lost and is found!" And they began to celebrate.

Gowan follows Ken Bailey's argument that the son did not truly repent. Instead, his request to "treat me like one of your hired hands" indicated his desire to remain independent, working for his father as a "contractor" and living

---

24. Bruce D. Chilton, "Jesus and the Repentance of E. P. Sanders," *Tyndale Bulletin* 39 (1988): 4.

wherever he chose. Gowan thus surmises that God's forgiveness does not depend on one's repentance.[25]

However, this view is problematic on three counts. First, though independent, a hired hand is not in a financially secure position, since he is employed at the will of the master. Instead, the son was expressing humility by offering to be treated as one of his father's workers.

Second, the context indicates that the son did repent. He confessed his sin twice, saying, "I have sinned against heaven and before you" (15:18, 21). He showed he meant it by going back to his father (15:18, 20).[26] Nolland notes that though the son's repentance was motivated by his desire to improve his pitiful state, it was no less a penitence. It is often the painful consequences of sin that bring us to our senses. The son's inner thoughts showed that he was not merely wrangling for free meals but experienced remorse, saying that he was no longer worthy to be called a son and seeking to make restitution by working for his father. Moreover, the son's repentance is anticipated by the teaching in the preceding two parables.

Third, the parable does not tell us that the father extended forgiveness when the son was in the far country. We see his compassionate response only when the son was on his way back.[27] God's forgiveness can be experienced the moment we turn to him. The father longed for the son's return, but the embrace of restoration could be given only when the son was on his way home.[28]

2. The Pharisee and the Tax Collector (Luke 18:9–14)

> [9] He also told this parable to some who trusted in themselves that they were righteous and regarded others with contempt: [10] "Two men went up to the temple to pray, one a Pharisee and the other a tax-collector. [11] The Pharisee, standing by himself, was praying thus, 'God, I thank you that I am not like other people: thieves, rogues, adulterers, or even like this tax-collector. [12] I fast twice

---

25. Gowan, *Bible and Forgiveness*, 142; Ken E. Bailey, *Poet and Peasant and Through Peasant Eyes: A Literary-Cultural Approach to the Parables in Luke* (Grand Rapids: Eerdmans, 1983), 173–76.

26. O. E. Hofius compares this to faithless Israel's resolve to return to her first husband in Hos 2:7 ("Altestamentliche Motive im Gleichnis vom verlorenen Sohn," *New Testament Studies* 24 [1977–78]: 241, cited in Nolland, *Luke 9:21 – 18:34*, 784).

27. Edwards, *Luke*, 442.

28. So also Bash writes, "When the son returned, the father forgave the son and gave him a new start" (*Just Forgiveness*, 33).

a week; I give a tenth of all my income.' [13] But the tax-collector, standing far off, would not even look up to heaven, but was beating his breast and saying, 'God, be merciful to me, a sinner!' [14] I tell you, this man went down to his home justified rather than the other; for all who exalt themselves will be humbled, but all who humble themselves will be exalted."

According to his view that God initiates forgiveness before repentance, Gowan uses this parable to say that "God graciously offers forgiveness to those who in no way can claim to deserve it."[29] If we follow this reasoning, then God should also offer the same forgiveness to the self-righteous Pharisee. Rather, it is more accurate to say that God's justification is given to the one who recognized his own sinfulness and asked for the mercy of forgiveness. Only the tax collector embodied the contrition of Psalm 51:1, "Have mercy on me, O God."[30]

3. Zacchaeus (Luke 19:1–10)

[1] He entered Jericho and was passing through it. [2] A man was there named Zacchaeus; he was a chief tax-collector and was rich. [3] He was trying to see who Jesus was, but on account of the crowd he could not, because he was short in stature. [4] So he ran ahead and climbed a sycamore tree to see him, because he was going to pass that way. [5] When Jesus came to the place, he looked up and said to him, "Zacchaeus, hurry and come down; for I must stay at your house today." [6] So he hurried down and was happy to welcome him. [7] All who saw it began to grumble and said, "He has gone to be the guest of one who is a sinner." [8] Zacchaeus stood there and said to the Lord, "Look, half of my possessions, Lord, I will give to the poor; and if I have defrauded anyone of anything, I will pay back four times as much." [9] Then Jesus said to him, "Today salvation has come to this house, because he too is a son of Abraham. [10] For the Son of Man came to seek out and to save the lost."

Some scholars argue that this is not a story about salvation but an affirmation of Zacchaeus's righteousness. This interpretation hinges on the Greek present tense in Zacchaeus's statement, which may be understood as a habitual act – that is, "I have been giving to the poor . . . I have been paying back four times

---

29. Gowan, *Bible and Forgiveness*, 139.
30. Edwards, *Luke*, 505.

as much" (19:8). Jesus's pronouncement of Zacchaeus' salvation is then a public vindication of a man shunned by the townspeople.[31]

However, the Greek present tense can also be understood as the "present of anticipation"; that is to say, Zacchaeus is so certain of what he is going to do that he expresses it in the present tense.[32] Such an interpretation would make better sense because it would be strange if Zacchaeus were in the habit of defrauding people and then paying them back. In any case, Jesus identified Zacchaeus as one of the "lost" (19:10), meaning he was estranged from God. Although faith is not explicitly stated, it is demonstrated by Zacchaeus's actions: he sought out Jesus, welcomed him into his house, and promised acts of charity and compensation.[33] While there is no mention of forgiveness, Zechariah's psalm in Luke 1:77 shows that forgiveness is synonymous with salvation: "to give knowledge of *salvation* to his people by the *forgiveness* of their sins."[34] Therefore, to declare salvation in the context of Luke's gospel is also to pronounce forgiveness.

Luke also regularly made repentance a prerequisite of forgiveness, as seen in the following verses:[35]

- John the Baptist's preaching (Luke 3:3): "He went into all the region around the Jordan, proclaiming a baptism of *repentance* for the *forgiveness* of sins."
- Jesus's commission to his disciples (Luke 24:47): ". . . and that *repentance* and *forgiveness* of sins is to be proclaimed in his name to all nations, beginning from Jerusalem."
- Peter's preaching at Pentecost (Acts 2:38): "Peter said to them, '*Repent*, and be baptized every one of you in the name of Jesus Christ so that your sins may be *forgiven*; and you will receive the gift of the Holy Spirit.'"
- Peter's preaching to the Jewish council (Acts 5:31): "God exalted him at his right hand as Leader and Saviour, so that he might give *repentance* to Israel and *forgiveness* of sins."

---

31. Green, *Luke*, 672–73; Joseph A. Fitzmyer, *The Gospel according to Luke X–XXIV*, AB (New York: Doubleday, 1985), 1220, 1225.

32. Smyth §1879; also Stein, *Luke*, 466; Bock, *Luke 9:51 – 24:53*, 1520.

33. Nolland, *Luke 18:35 – 24:53*, 906, explains that the fourfold restitution went beyond the Jewish law (Lev 6:2–5; Exod 22:1–4) but followed the Roman law.

34. Gowan, *Bible and Forgiveness*, 127.

35. Bash, *Just Forgiveness*, 151, n. 10.

- Peter's rebuke to Simon the magician (Acts 8:22): "*Repent* therefore of this wickedness of yours, and pray to the Lord that, if possible, the intent of your heart may be *forgiven* you."
- Paul's preaching to King Agrippa (Acts 26:18): ". . . to open their eyes so that they may *turn* from darkness to light and from the power of Satan to God, so that they may receive *forgiveness* of sins and a place among those who are sanctified by faith in me."

The necessity of repentance is also demonstrated in the Epistles, which we will look at next.

4. In the Corinthian Church (2 Cor 2:5–11)

> ⁵ But if anyone has caused pain, he has caused it not to me, but to some extent – not to exaggerate it – to all of you. ⁶ This punishment by the majority is enough for such a person; ⁷ so now instead you should forgive and console him, so that he may not be overwhelmed by excessive sorrow [*lupē*]. ⁸ So I urge you to reaffirm your love for him. ⁹ I wrote for this reason: to test you and to know whether you are obedient in everything. ¹⁰ Anyone whom you forgive, I also forgive. What I have forgiven, if I have forgiven anything, has been for your sake in the presence of Christ. ¹¹ And we do this so that we may not be outwitted by Satan; for we are not ignorant of his designs.

In this situation, Paul advocated for the forgiveness of an offender,[36] stating that the offender had experienced sorrow (*lupē*). This is a word that Paul uses again in 2 Corinthians 7:9–10 in relation to repentance:

> As it is, I rejoice, not because you were grieved [*lupeō*], but because you were grieved [*lupeō*] into repenting. For you felt a godly grief [*lupeō*], so that you suffered no loss through us.
>
> For godly grief [*lupē*] produces a repentance that leads to salvation without regret, whereas worldly grief [*lupē*] produces death. (ESV)

---

36. The offender may have been the reprobate of 1 Cor 5:1–2 who had a sexual relationship with his stepmother and whom Paul said should be disciplined. However, we cannot be certain of this.

Godly grief leads to repentance, and it is on this basis that Paul calls on the Corinthian church to restore the offender to its fellowship.[37]

5. If We Confess Our Sins (1 John 1:9)

> If we confess our sins, he is faithful and just to forgive us our sins and to cleanse us from all unrighteousness. (ESV)

John's first epistle deals with whether the gift of new life in Christ means that Christians must never or cannot sin again. John answers that we cannot claim that we have no sin (1:8, 10), but forgiveness is available whenever we confess.[38] John is not dealing with justification but ongoing sanctification and discipleship. If God requires confession, and we are to forgive like him, then forgiveness ought to be conditional on repentance.

Conclusion

Bash discusses an incident where Christians were expected to forgive heinous crimes:

> In 1992, an IRA bomb in London had the incidental effect of destroying much of St Helen's Church, Bishopsgate, London. The Rector, Prebendary R. C. Lucas, was asked in a television interview whether he had forgiven the bombers. His answer was, "I'm not aware that anyone has asked for forgiveness." Lucas' deft reply rightly assumes that repentance should precede forgiveness.[39]

Similarly, Villanueva recounts a day in 2009 when the Philippines gained the infamous record of having the greatest number of journalists killed in a single day in the midst of an election. A reporter asked the wife of one of those killed whether she had forgiven the perpetrators. The woman said, "Even if I forgive them, I no longer have a husband who would come home and embrace me."

---

37. Paul Barnett, *The Second Epistle to the Corinthians*, NICNT (Grand Rapids: Eerdmans, 1997), 132, writes that reconciliation is not only for the transgressor's welfare but also for the church's unity against Satan's disruption. There needs to be both discipline and restoration for the church's well-being.

38. Gowan, *Bible and Forgiveness*, 191, argues that forgiveness is offered at God's initiative. However, the phrase "if we confess," using the Greek subjunctive, shows that forgiveness, while assured on God's character, is dependent on the condition of confessing our sins.

39. Bash, *Just Forgiveness*, 151, n. 12.

In other words, there is a yearning for justice, and Villanueva concludes that though it may not happen in this life, it will, for sure, happen in the next.[40]

Unlike the reporters, we need to ask the right question first: not whether the victims have forgiven, but whether the violators have repented. Bash gives four reasons why unconditional forgiveness is not helpful. First, it leaves the wrongdoer free from accountability. For example, a pastor counselled a wife to forgive her unfaithful husband but did not deal with the man for his adultery. Naturally, there was no change, and the disillusioned wife left the church and divorced her husband.

Second, the injured party may say he or she wishes to forgive without confronting, which robs the other person of the opportunity to make amends and be reconciled. Such avoidance will probably result in a tense relationship, thus adding to unresolved stress.

Third, the conflict may be entirely a misunderstanding, so there is nothing to forgive. It would be better to clarify matters than to nurse bitterness. Worse, when a supposed victim announces that he or she forgives a clueless wrongdoer, the "victim" accuses the other person of guilt without proof.

Fourth, it violates the victim's sense of justice. "Since many victims feel violated, it would be an additional burden on them if they believed they ought to forgive the very people who had violated them and who were unrepentant."[41] An insistence on unconditional forgiveness also affects the victim's self-worth by implying that the victim can let others take advantage of him or her with impunity.

I would add a fifth reason: that it undermines the character of God. Unconditional forgiveness implies that God does not care about righteousness. In the next chapter, on forgiveness in the OT, the grace and justice of God will be seen even more clearly.

40. Villanueva, It's OK to Be Not OK, 93.
41. Bash, "Difficult Texts," 277–78; Michaels, John, 495.

4

What Is Forgiveness in the Old Testament?

A husband had a one-night stand. The wife was heartbroken and considered leaving him. After his tearful repentance and a painful counselling process, the wife felt convicted by God to forgive him and save the marriage.

However, a few months later, the man lamented to me that his wife was constantly questioning his whereabouts. I told him to bear fruit worthy of repentance by taking the initiative to be accountable for all his activities, whether online or offline. Trust takes time to rebuild. Did she forgive him? Yes, by the very act of taking him back. Were there consequences? Yes, he suffered the loss of intimacy and independence. However, as he committed to a renewal of his life, their marriage is stronger today.

In the OT, there is often an emphasis on the consequences of sin, even when there is forgiveness. The first part of this chapter focuses on God's forgiveness in five narratives:

- Cain
- The golden calf
- Israel's refusal to enter the promised land
- David's adultery and murder
- David's census-taking

We will see that God's forgiveness is dependent on repentance, but there may still be discipline for the sin.

In the second part, we will look at three texts on human forgiveness, which will show the need for genuine repentance:

- Joseph and his brothers
- Moses and Pharaoh
- Samuel's rejection of Saul

God's Forgiveness
1. Cain (Gen 4:1–16)

¹ Now the man knew his wife Eve, and she conceived and bore Cain, saying, "I have produced a man with the help of the LORD." ² Next she bore his brother Abel. Now Abel was a keeper of sheep, and Cain a tiller of the ground. ³ In the course of time Cain brought to the LORD an offering of the fruit of the ground, ⁴ and Abel for his part brought of the firstlings of his flock, their fat portions. And the LORD had regard for Abel and his offering, ⁵ but for Cain and his offering he had no regard. So Cain was very angry, and his countenance fell. ⁶ The LORD said to Cain, "Why are you angry, and why has your countenance fallen? ⁷ If you do well, will you not be accepted? And if you do not do well, sin is lurking at the door; its desire is for you, but you must master it."[1]

⁸ Cain said to his brother Abel, "Let us go out to the field." And when they were in the field, Cain rose up against his brother Abel and killed him. ⁹ Then the LORD said to Cain, "Where is your brother Abel?" He said, "I do not know; am I my brother's keeper?" ¹⁰ And the LORD said, "What have you done? Listen; your brother's blood is crying out to me from the ground! ¹¹ And now you are cursed from the ground, which has opened its mouth to receive your brother's blood from your hand. ¹² When you till the ground, it will no longer yield to you its strength; you will be a fugitive and a wanderer on the earth." ¹³ Cain said to the LORD, "My punishment is greater than I can bear! ¹⁴ Today you have driven me away from the soil, and I shall be hidden from your face; I shall be a fugitive and a wanderer on the earth, and anyone who meets me may kill me." ¹⁵ Then the LORD said to him, "Not so! Whoever kills Cain will suffer a sevenfold vengeance." And the LORD put a mark on Cain, so that no one who came upon him would kill him. ¹⁶ Then Cain went away from the presence of the LORD, and settled in the land of Nod, east of Eden.

---

1. An observation can be made about anger from this verse. God accepted Abel's offering because he brought the firstlings of his flock, while Cain merely offered fruits, not firstfruits, from the ground (4:3–4). So also Gordon Wenham, *Genesis 1–15*, WBC (Waco: Word), 103. Thus, God's admonishment to Cain "to do well" (4:7) may be telling him both to offer his best to God and to master his resentment. This advice shows that anger in itself is not sinful. Emotions are not wrong, but it becomes sinful when one keeps harbouring anger or acts harmfully.

It seems that there was no forgiveness for Cain in this tragic story, though he was not punished as severely as he might have been.[2] However, I will show that Cain did repent and was forgiven but had to bear the consequences of his crime.

Whether Cain repented turns on the interpretation of Genesis 4:13, which more literally in Hebrew is, "My punishment ['avon] is too great to bear [nasa']!" Was Cain complaining about God's punishment, which is the usual translation, or was he confessing his guilt? Both interpretations are possible in Hebrew because 'avon can mean punishment or guilt, and nasa' can mean bear or forgive in the sense of bearing away sins (e.g. Exod 34:7; Ps 85:2; Isa 33:24). Therefore, Cain could be saying, "My guilt is too great to forgive." John H. Sailhamer argues that this interpretation explains why God protected Cain in 4:15. "The point of the narrative is that God forgives a repentant sinner."[3]

Cain's statement is not the only wordplay in this account: "Abel" means "breath" in Hebrew, and his life was as short as a breath; "Cain" means "gain" as explained by Eve, but ironically she lost both sons; Cain became a *nad* (wanderer) who settled in Nod. Thus, we can understand the double meaning in Genesis 4:13 as Cain both seeking forgiveness and fearing the punishment of his offence.[4]

---

2. Gowan, *Bible on Forgiveness*, 7. It is perplexing that God did not impose the death sentence for murder as required by Gen 9:6. Further, such a penalty cannot be commuted by a ransom (Num 35:31). A consideration is that the law may not yet have been applicable, since the punishment for murder was enacted only after the flood (Gen 6:11). Wenham, *Genesis 1–15*, 108, suggests that where there is a conflict of familial loyalties, expulsion is the appropriate punishment, citing Absalom's exile in 2 Sam 13–14 as an example.

3. John H. Sailhamer, "Genesis," in *Expositor's Bible Commentary*, Vol. 1, *Genesis–Leviticus* (Grand Rapids: Zondervan, 2008), 101. The Greek translates it as "to be forgiven." Wenham, *Genesis 1–15*, 108, argues that "bear" in relation to humans means paying the penalty for their sin, but when God "bears," it means forgiveness for the sinner. Wenham concludes that Cain is referring to the consequences of his iniquity. However, Cain's speech in 4:13 is ambivalent because he is speaking to the Lord, so "bear" may be referring to himself bearing his own punishment or to God forgiving his guilt.

The question is also raised whether Cain was truly repentant, since he built a city apparently to defend himself and named it after his son Enoch (4:17). However, there are various text-critical issues with this verse, and Wenham, *Genesis 1–15*, 93, 111, translates the verse as, "Then Cain knew his wife. She conceived and gave birth to Enoch. He (Enoch) was building a city and Enoch called the city after his son's name (Irad)."

4. The one who killed became afraid of being killed (*harag*). Kenneth A. Mathews, *Genesis 1–11:26*, NAC (Nashville: Broadman & Holman, 1996), 277, explains that *harag* frequently describes personal violence or warfare and is seldom used for God-authorized judicial execution. Cain, therefore, was terrified of getting murdered.

God's response in 4:15 in the English translations[5] is "Not so! Whoever kills Cain will suffer a sevenfold vengeance." This negation would address Cain's fear of being killed. However, in the Hebrew, God's reply begins with *laken*, which should be translated as "therefore," rather than "not so." Thus, God's answer would be, "*Therefore*, whoever kills Cain will suffer a sevenfold vengeance," making it a promise of God's protection in response to Cain's confession. Although the offender's remorse came only after his denial and God's sentencing, contrition still made a difference because the wrongdoer was not treated fully as he deserved.[6]

2. The Golden Calf (Exod 33–34)

> [4] When the people heard these harsh words, they mourned ['aval], and no one put on ornaments ['adi]. [5] For the LORD had said to Moses, "Say to the Israelites, 'You are a stiff-necked people; if for a single moment I should go up among you, I would consume you. So now take off your ornaments ['adi], and I will decide what to do to you.'" [6] Therefore the Israelites stripped themselves of their ornaments ['adi], from Mount Horeb onward. (33:4–6)

Does Exodus 33:4 indicate the people's repentance after their idolatry of the golden calf? Gowan's view is that this mourning did not constitute penitence and that God unconditionally forgave on his own initiative. However, I will show that putting away ornaments represented remorse, to which God responded with forgiveness.

Gowan thinks that "mourn" ('aval) was nothing more than regret. "Mourning" primarily refers to lamentation at death or destruction.[7] However,

---

5. The English translations follow the Greek emendation to "not so." Wenham, *Genesis 1–15*, 95, follows the Hebrew.

6. Gowan, *Bible on Forgiveness*, 7, does not see the mitigation as forgiveness because there was no reconciliation. However, God's mark on Cain would indicate that he still belonged to God.

7. Gowan, 14–15. He argues that 'aval (mourning) recurs in Num 14:39–40 after the people were consigned to the wilderness for forty years because they refused to enter the promised land. However, it was not a genuine repentance because they were not willing to accept God's punishment but tried to enter the promised land on their own and thus suffered defeat.

Hamilton points out a difference between the two accounts of mourning: in Exodus, it preceded, while in Numbers, it followed God's final judgment. Thus, the mourning in Exod 33 pointed to remorse at the potential loss of God's presence (Exod 33:3), but in Num 14, it was an act of rebellion against God's sentence (Victor P. Hamilton, *Exodus: An Exegetical Commentary* [Grand Rapids: Baker Academic, 2011], 559).

more significant is the removal of ornaments (*'adi*), which is repeated three times. Victor P. Hamilton notes that stripping oneself of jewellery may be a way of renouncing idolatry, as shown in Genesis 35:4: "So they gave to Jacob all the foreign gods that they had, and the rings that were in their ears; and Jacob hid them under the oak that was near Shechem." Douglas K. Stuart adds that removing jewellery reverses what the people did when they took off their gold to build the calf (Exod 32:2–4).[8]

After the mourning in Exodus 33, Moses asked for God's presence to be with them. This time, God agreed, and no further punishment was imposed. Thus, we can conclude that the debt of idolatry was cancelled, and the relationship was restored.

Yet, because God might still consume a stiff-necked people (33:3, 5), Moses requested to see God's glory, where his divine forgiving nature was proclaimed:

> The LORD, the LORD,
> a God merciful and gracious,
> slow to anger,
> and abounding in steadfast love and faithfulness,
> keeping steadfast love for the thousandth generation,
> forgiving [*nasa'*] iniquity and transgression and sin,
> yet by no means clearing the guilty,
> but visiting the iniquity of the parents
> upon the children
> and the children's children,
> to the third and the fourth generation. (34:6–7)

Because of who God is, forgiveness (*nasa'*) is possible. However, forgiveness does not remove the repercussions of sin. "It is not remission of punishment, as some definitions have it, but is the re-establishment of a broken relationship, while suffering as a consequence of sin does take place."[9] The reference to the third and fourth generations requires some explanation. It does not mean that God punishes the innocent descendants, which would contradict the principle of individual retribution in Ezekiel 18. Rather, it refers to the consequences of sin that will affect all the generations living in a household, especially if they

---

8. Hamilton, *Exodus*, 558; Stuart, *Exodus*, 693, notes that jewellery was not worn from Horeb onwards (Exod 33:6) as a sign of turning away from idolatry.

9. Gowan, *Bible and Forgiveness*, 19.

emulate that sin. Based on the average lifespan, there would usually be three and not more than four generations living together.[10]

Based on this self-revelation of God, Moses sought confirmation of God's presence: "If now I have found favour in your sight, O LORD, I pray, let the LORD go with us. Although this is a stiff-necked people, pardon [*salakh*] our iniquity and our sin, and take us for your inheritance" (34:9). In this verse, Moses uses a different term for pardon – not the usual *nasa'*, but *salakh*. I will discuss this more extensively in the following Numbers 14 passage, but essentially, it is a term related to the covenant, indicated by Moses's request that God take the people as his inheritance. In the rest of Exodus 34, God made a covenant again with the people, showing that forgiveness led to a restored relationship.

3. Israel's Refusal to Enter the Promised Land (Num 14)

[19] "Forgive [*salakh*] the iniquity of this people according to the greatness of your steadfast love, just as you have pardoned [*nasa'*] this people, from Egypt even until now."

[20] Then the LORD said, "I do forgive [*salakh*], just as you have asked; [21] nevertheless – as I live, and as all the earth shall be filled with the glory of the LORD – [22] none of the people who have seen my glory and the signs that I did in Egypt and in the wilderness, and yet have tested me these ten times and have not obeyed my voice, [23] shall see the land that I swore to give to their ancestors; none of those who despised me shall see it." (14:19–23)

Did God forgive the people before they repented? When they refused to enter the promised land, God threatened to destroy them and start over with Moses (14:12). However, Moses implored God to forgive (*salakh*) and pardon (*nasa'*) the people. The Lord responded that he would *salakh*, but glaringly omitted *nasa'* (14:20). Judgment was then announced: everyone would die in the desert, except for Joshua, Caleb, and those below twenty years of age (14:30–33).

Does *salakh* mean forgiveness then?[11] It is better understood as an act of divine grace to continue in a relationship with the people without the forgiveness of sin. Whereas *salakh* is at God's initiative, *nasa'* requires

---

10. Gowan, 20; Stuart, *Exodus*, 717.

11. Gowan, 20, 25, does not see a difference between *salakh* and *nasa'*. He argues that forgiveness should not be understood in the narrow sense of exoneration of sin or annulment of punishment but as the continuation of the covenant relationship.

repentance. Jacob Milgrom gives the example of Amos 7:2–3 where *salakh* is synonymous with "relent" – God temporarily halted his punishment against Israel to give them a chance to repent.[12] K. D. Sakenfeld explains *salakh* as God preserving the community without lifting specific punishments.[13] As with a parent-child relationship, a blood tie cannot be denied, but the dynamics of the bond vary with the parties' behaviour. Parents may punish an unrepentant child, but that child still belongs to them as their offspring.

God's agreement to *salakh* but not *nasa'* brought judgment on the older generation. Instead of accepting this decree in repentance, the people made a belated attempt to enter the promised land against Moses's advice. Such continued rebellion showed that their repentance was false, so there was no *nasa'* and no escape from punishment.[14]

4. David's Adultery and Murder (2 Sam 12)

> [7]Nathan said to David, "You are the man! Thus says the LORD, the God of Israel: I anointed you king over Israel, and I rescued you from the hand of Saul; [8]I gave you your master's house, and your master's wives into your bosom, and gave you the house of Israel and of Judah; and if that had been too little, I would have added as much more. [9]Why have you despised the word of the LORD, to do what is evil in his sight? You have struck down Uriah the Hittite with the sword, and have taken his wife to be your wife, and have killed him with the sword of the Ammonites. [10]Now therefore the sword shall never depart from your house, for you have despised me, and have taken the wife of Uriah the Hittite to be your wife. [11]Thus says the LORD: I will raise up trouble against you from

---

12. Jacob Milgrom, *Numbers*, JPS Torah Commentary (Philadelphia: Jewish Publication Society of America, 1989), 396. J. Hausmann, "סלח," *TDOT* 10:263, points out that Isa 55:7 relates *salakh* to the Davidic covenant, and Jer 31:34 relates it to the new covenant.

13. K. D. Sakenfeld, "The Problem of Divine Forgiveness in Numbers 14," *Catholic Biblical Quarterly* 37 (1975): 327. Hausmann, *TDOT* 10:262, notes that *salakh* is connected with repentance in 2 Chr 7:14 and Isa 55:7. However, it can also be seen that repentance brings more than preservation of the community for there is also healing of land in 2 Chr 7:14 and God's compassion in Isa 55:7.

14. It may be that Moses used *salakh* and *nasa'* as parallel terms in Num 14:19, but from God's reply, *nasa'* is a broader term that would include *salakh*, since with repentance and forgiveness there would be a restoration of the relationship. However, *salakh* by itself would mean a gracious continuation of a relationship, even if there was no repentance, but judgment would still be imposed.

within your own house; and I will take your wives before your eyes, and give them to your neighbour, and he shall lie with your wives in the sight of this very sun. [12] For you did it secretly; but I will do this thing before all Israel, and before the sun." [13] David said to Nathan, "I have sinned against the LORD." Nathan said to David, "Now the LORD has put away your sin; you shall not die. [14] Nevertheless, because by this deed you have utterly scorned the LORD, the child that is born to you shall die." [15] Then Nathan went to his house. (12:7–15)

This episode clearly shows that repentance is the condition for forgiveness. As a result, there was remission of the expected death penalty, although there were immediate and long-term consequences for the sin. However, three puzzling issues remain: (1) Why did David confess that he had sinned only against the LORD? (2) How could the mandatory death penalty for murder be commuted? (3) Was it fair that David's child died in his place?

First, why did David mention only the Lord in his confession? After all, he caused harm to Bathsheba and Uriah. It seems that the biblical writer focused on the theological root of sin. In Nathan's oracle, God indicted David twice for despising his word and himself (2 Sam 12:9–10). "Had David not rebelled against the Lord's Word, these people would not have been murdered or abused."[15]

In response to David's confession, God took away[16] his sin and declared that David would not die. According to the Torah, adultery and murder incurred the death penalty, and the death sentence for murder could not be commuted by a ransom (Num 35:31). So, the second question is how could God rescind a capital punishment? It should be stressed that David had been convicted and condemned, but God had the sovereign right to overturn a death sentence. Today, this concept is reflected by presidential pardons exercised under the constitution. That David is spared at God's discretion is emphasized by the Hebrew syntax in 12:13, where the subject "LORD" is placed first in the sentence rather than the usual verb. It is, therefore, better translated as,

---

15. Robert D. Bergen, *1, 2 Samuel*, NAC (Nashville: Broadman & Holman, 1996), 373. Obviously, David cannot confess to Uriah who is dead. As for Bathsheba, the text is silent about whether she was a consenting party to David's sins.

16. "Take away" is the *hiphil* (causative Hebrew stem) of *'avar*, which is used as a parallel for *nasa'* in Job 7:21, "Why do you not pardon [*nasa'*] my transgression and take away [*hiphil* of *'avar*] my iniquity?" In all six occurrences, it refers to divine forgiveness (2 Sam 12:13; 24:20//1 Chr 21:8; Job 7:21; Zech 3:4; Jer 11:15), while *nasa'* can be used for human forgiveness as well, e.g. in 1 Samuel (1 Sam 15:25; 25:28).

"Indeed, it is the LORD himself who has put away your sin; you shall not die." The remission of punishment is entirely at God's pleasure.

The third issue is most perplexing: how could God take the life of an innocent child because of the father's sin? Some have explained this based on the ancient concept of corporate responsibility – that is, a community is held responsible for the sin of any one of its members.[17] However, there are problems with this understanding, not least of which is the Deuteronomic principle, "Parents shall not be put to death for their children, nor shall children be put to death for their parents; only for their own crimes may persons be put to death" (Deut 24:16).[18]

Most modern scholars distinguish between culpability and consequence – that is, a child is not held guilty for the parent's sin, but the child may suffer the consequences of such wrongdoing. Examples are children orphaned when a parent is incarcerated or made ill by an adult's cigarette smoke.[19] Therefore, David's illegitimate child is not held culpable but is an innocent victim of David's sin. David Daube offers an astute explanation, which he calls "ruler punishment": "the wrong committed by a ruler is repaid to him by a move against those under his rule, by taking away or damaging his free subjects."[20] Just as an owner is punished by taking away his or her property, so a king is punished by destroying his subjects. In David's case, his harem and his child are taken away. The child is not at fault, but the king must pay for scorning the Lord's honour (12:14).

5. David's Census-Taking (2 Sam 24)

[1] Again the anger of the LORD was kindled against Israel, and he incited David against them, saying, "Go, count the people of Israel and Judah."[21] [2] So the king said to Joab and the commanders of

---

17. A. A. Anderson, *2 Samuel*, WBC (Dallas: Word, 1989), 163.

18. See Maggie Sau Sen Choo, "Generational Sin: An Examination of the Corporate Retribution Formula in Exodus 20:5 in Relation to the "Sour Grapes" Proverb in Jeremiah 31 and Ezekiel 18" (MTh thesis, Regent College, Vancouver, 1999).

19. Bill T. Arnold, *1 & 2 Samuel*, NIVAC (Grand Rapids: Zondervan, 2003), 536; Mary J. Evans, *1 and 2 Samuel*, NIBCOT (Peabody: Hendrickson, 2000), 190.

20. David Daube, *Studies in Biblical Law* (New York: Cambridge University Press, 1947), 163. David Daube also used this principle to explain why David's people suffered for his census-taking in 2 Sam 24, although they were "innocent sheep."

21. The divine wrath was probably due to the people's rejection of God by demanding a human king. The prophet Samuel had warned them that a king would conscript their sons into his army (1 Sam 9:11–12), among other demands. Later, at Saul's royal anointing, the prophet

the army, who were with him, "Go through all the tribes of Israel, from Dan to Beer-sheba, and take a census of the people, so that I may know how many there are." . . .

¹⁰ But afterwards, David was stricken to the heart because he had numbered the people. David said to the LORD, "I have sinned greatly in what I have done. But now, O LORD, I pray you, take away²² the guilt of your servant; for I have done very foolishly." ¹¹ When David rose in the morning, the word of the LORD came to the prophet Gad, David's seer, saying, ¹² "Go and say to David: Thus says the LORD: Three things I offer you; choose one of them, and I will do it to you." ¹³ So Gad came to David and told him; he asked him, "Shall three years of famine come to you on your land? Or will you flee for three months before your foes while they pursue you? Or shall there be three days' pestilence in your land? Now consider, and decide what answer I shall return to the one who sent me." ¹⁴ Then David said to Gad, "I am in great distress; let us fall into the hand of the LORD, for his mercy is great; but let me not fall into human hands."

¹⁵ So the LORD sent a pestilence on Israel from that morning until the appointed time; and seventy thousand of the people died, from Dan to Beer-sheba. ¹⁶ But when the angel stretched out his hand towards Jerusalem to destroy it, the LORD relented concerning the evil, and said to the angel who was bringing destruction among the people, "It is enough; now stay your hand." The angel of the LORD was then by the threshing-floor of Araunah the Jebusite. ¹⁷ When David saw the angel who was destroying the people, he said to the LORD, "I alone have sinned, and I alone have done wickedly; but these sheep, what have they done? Let your hand, I pray, be against me and against my father's house."

¹⁸ That day Gad came to David and said to him, "Go up and erect an altar to the LORD on the threshing-floor of Araunah the Jebusite." ¹⁹ Following Gad's instructions, David went up, as the LORD had commanded. . . .

---

denounced the people's desire for a king as a great wickedness (1 Sam 12:17). Thus, though David said that the people were innocent in 2 Sam 24:17, this was true only with regard to the census-taking. The people were not completely guiltless in relation to God, and the taking of a census fulfilled the warning about the king forcing the people to work or fight for him. (1 Chr 21:1 attributes the instigation to *satan* or an accuser.)

22. "Take away" is the *hiphil* of *'avar*. See n. 16 above.

[24] . . . The king said to Araunah, ". . . I will buy them [the threshing-floor and oxen] from you for a price; I will not offer burnt-offerings to the LORD my God that cost me nothing." So David bought the threshing-floor and the oxen for fifty shekels of silver. [25] David built there an altar to the LORD, and offered burnt-offerings and offerings of well-being. So the LORD answered his supplication for the land, and the plague was averted from Israel. (24:1–2, 10–19, 24–25)

God seems particularly harsh in this narrative, for despite David's confession, God brought a severe disaster on the people. At this late stage of David's life, the king had to learn that repentance consisted not only of heartfelt words but also of restitution and renewal of life.

First, we have to understand what was wrong with taking a census. There are two possible explanations. One is that David did not collect the half-shekel ransom from each male, which was required by the Torah (Exod 30:11–16). Failure to do so would bring a plague (Exod 30:12). The second possible reason is David's pride in wanting to know how large his army was. The two reasons are related in that the ransom to be collected showed that the people belonged to God and not to the king. The death toll reducing his military might would thus be a fitting rebuke for the king. As Anderson puts it, "The king and the people should not rely on their own strength but they should depend on Yahweh."[23]

After taking the census, David was stricken by guilt and confessed in 24:10, but God responded by offering a choice of disasters. Unlike his word brought by Nathan in 1 Samuel 12, God did not declare any forgiveness. The second question then is why did God exact punishment despite David's confession? It seems that God expected something more.

A pestilence was sent on Israel from morning until "the appointed time" (24:15). It is not clear what "the appointed time" refers to, but it must be less than the specified three days because God relented (24:16), and the plague was later averted (24:25).[24] At that merciful pause, David made a further confession: "I alone have sinned, and I alone have done wickedly; but these sheep, what have they done? Let your hand, I pray, be against me and against my father's house" (24:17). In this second confession, the king now asked for the people to be spared. Rather than exploiting his population, he offered

---

23. Anderson, *2 Samuel*, 284.

24. Anderson, 286. The Septuagint reads it as "dinner time," implying that it was only for a day.

himself as a sacrifice. Repentance requires a willingness to accept one's penalty as restitution.

God then sent Gad with further instructions to erect an altar on Araunah's threshing-floor. Despite Araunah's offer of his land, David purchased it at his own cost. After the king made burnt- and peace-offerings,[25] the plague ended. In this last episode, David showed renewed change, for though he could have taken the land by his authority, he personally paid a commoner for it. Whereas he started with pride in taking a census, the king now learned to worship the Almighty and serve the people. Divine forgiveness depended on David's full repentance.

Human Forgiveness

We will look at three[26] requests for human forgiveness in the OT that use *nasa'*: Joseph's brothers in Genesis 50, Pharaoh in Exodus 10, and Saul in 1 Samuel 15. Only Joseph's brothers were given a positive response; the other two were rejected because of their hypocritical repentance.

1. Joseph and His Brothers (Gen 50:15–21)

> [15] Realizing that their father was dead, Joseph's brothers said, "What if Joseph still bears a grudge against us and pays us back in full for all the wrong that we did to him?" [16] So they approached Joseph, saying, "Your father gave this instruction before he died, [17] 'Say to Joseph: I beg you, forgive [*nasa'*] the crime of your brothers and the wrong they did in harming you.' Now therefore please forgive [*nasa'*] the crime of the servants of the God of your father." Joseph

---

25. Tony W. Cartledge, *1 & 2 Samuel*, SHBC (Macon: Smyth & Helwys, 2001), 711, explains that burnt-offerings may have had an expiatory purpose (Lev 9:7; 14:20) and were associated with petitions to God (1 Sam 13:12). Peace-offerings functioned to maintain good relations between God and the worshippers, with the meat shared by the priests and people.

26. A fourth text, regarding David and Abigail (1 Sam 25), is omitted because *nasa'* is used there only as a formality. When Abigail met David, she said, "Upon me alone, my lord, be the guilt; please let your servant speak in your ears, and hear the words of your servant" (25:24). When she spoke further, she said, "Please forgive [*nasa'*] the trespass of your servant" (25:28). However, Abigail was not at fault, because, as she explained, "But I, your servant, did not see the young men of my lord, whom you sent" (25:25). Kyle P. McCarter, Jr., *1 Samuel*, AB (Garden City: Doubleday, 1980), 398, explains the expression as a polite way of initiating a conversation with a superior, as in 2 Sam 14:9. It simply means, "Let any burden of blame that might arise from our conversation rest upon me and not you!" I see it as saying, "Excuse me," or "Sorry to interrupt," in today's context.

wept when they spoke to him. [18] Then his brothers also wept, fell down before him, and said, "We are here as your slaves." [19] But Joseph said to them, "Do not be afraid! Am I in the place of God? [20] Even though you intended to do harm to me, God intended it for good, in order to preserve a numerous people, as he is doing today. [21] So have no fear; I myself will provide for you and your little ones." In this way he reassured them, speaking kindly to them.

Joseph's brothers repented in the above incident, but two issues may be raised. First, had Joseph already forgiven them unconditionally in Genesis 45? Second, were there any consequences following their repentance?

In Genesis 45, when Joseph revealed himself to his brothers, his pardon was demonstrated through his tears, kisses, and embrace, even though his brothers had uttered no remorse. However, their repentance was shown in the preceding chapter when the brothers interceded for Benjamin, who had been falsely accused. Judah even offered to remain as a slave in place of Benjamin (Gen 44:33), reversing what the brothers had done in selling off Joseph as a slave. When Judah offered this restitution, Joseph revealed himself to his siblings. He forgave when there were signs of repentance, though the brothers' guilty consciences must have weighed on them till they made a full confession in Genesis 50.

Second, were there any consequences for the brothers? Perhaps the weight of their guilt was punishment enough.[27] Furthermore, Hamilton suggests that Joseph's question, "Am I in the place of God?" could mean, "Am I in God's place to impose retribution? Vengeance is Yahweh's. He will repay, if necessary" (cf. Deut 32:35; Rom 11:19).[28] In other words, with demonstrated repentance, any repercussions are left to God.[29]

2. Moses and Pharaoh (Exod 10:16–20)

[16] Pharaoh hurriedly summoned Moses and Aaron and said, "I have sinned against the LORD your God, and against you. [17] Do forgive [nasa'] my sin just this once, and pray to the LORD your God that at the least he remove this deadly thing from me." [18] So

---

27. Victor P. Hamilton, *Genesis 18–50*, NICOT (Grand Rapids: Eerdmans, 1995), 705, notes that Joseph did not say, "I forgive you," in Gen 50 because he had already forgiven them.

28. Hamilton, *Genesis 18–50*, 705.

29. Kenneth A. Mathews, *Genesis 11:27 – 50:26*, NAC (Nashville: Broadman & Holman, 2005), 927, writes that "Joesph cannot usurp deity's designs."

he went out from Pharaoh and prayed to the LORD. [19] The LORD
changed the wind into a very strong west wind, which lifted the
locusts and drove them into the Red Sea; not a single locust was
left in all the country of Egypt. [20] But [Hebrew "And"] the LORD
hardened Pharaoh's heart, and he would not let the Israelites go.

After the eighth plague of locusts, Pharaoh admitted his sin and asked for
forgiveness, but said nothing about releasing the Israelites. There was no
change, only a desperate plea to avoid "this deadly thing." In fact, the hardening
of Pharaoh's heart could be considered part of God's punishment. Although
10:20 is translated with a "but" in the English versions, the Hebrew syntax
should be translated "and," that is, the hardening was part of God's response
to Pharaoh's fake confession, knowing that he had no intention to obey. So,
God sent the ninth plague of darkness over the land of Egypt.

3. Saul and Samuel (1 Sam 15:25)

[24] Saul said to Samuel, "I have sinned; for I have transgressed the
commandment of the LORD and your words, because I feared the
people and obeyed their voice. [25] Now therefore, I pray, pardon
[*nasa'*] my sin, and return with me, so that I may worship the
LORD." [26] Samuel said to Saul, "I will not return with you; for you
have rejected the word of the LORD, and the LORD has rejected
you from being king over Israel." [27] As Samuel turned to go away,
Saul caught hold of the hem of his robe, and it tore. [28] And Samuel
said to him, "The LORD has torn the kingdom of Israel from you
this very day, and has given it to a neighbour of yours, who is
better than you. [29] Moreover the Glory of Israel will not recant or
change his mind; for he is not a mortal, that he should change his
mind." [30] Then Saul said, "I have sinned; yet honour me now before
the elders of my people and before Israel, and return with me, so
that I may worship the LORD your God." [31] So Samuel turned back
after Saul; and Saul worshipped the LORD.

Samuel and the LORD rejected Saul's confession because he was not remorseful
despite his words. Instead of taking responsibility for his sin, he blamed the
people twice (15:15, 21), when Saul himself wanted to spare King Agag and
the best of the animals (15:9). Little wonder that Samuel denounced Saul for
being rebellious and stubborn (15:23). Saul made his first "confession" in 15:24
only when Samuel avowed God's rejection of him as king, but even then, he

gave a lame excuse of fearing the people's demand. Thus, Samuel reiterated God's rejection of Saul.

Saul then made a second "confession" in 15:30, but his motivation was only to beg Samuel to return with him to preserve his honour before the people. His detachment from God is shown by referring to the Lord as Samuel's God, not his own. "Instead of honouring God, Saul is concerned with honouring himself."[30] Arnold calls this a "self-serving confession," with no indication that the king will act differently in the future.[31]

From Saul's downfall, we learn that two elements are necessary for a genuine confession: not to make excuses, and to have the right motivation – that is, to want to obey God rather than simply to avoid the consequences.

Conclusion

All the above examples show that divine and human forgiveness depend on repentance. Such repentance consists of confession, a willingness to make restitution, and acts of renewal. We also see that true contrition may ameliorate the punishment, but there may still be consequences to bear.

It seems as if the OT is harsher than the NT because Jesus welcomed the lost without imposing further consequences. The difference is that the NT, especially the gospels, focuses on salvation or entry into the kingdom of God, while the OT is more concerned with sanctification or life in the kingdom of God. However, the same principle of forgiveness coupled with discipline is also found in the NT. Paul experienced this in 2 Corinthians 12:7–8 when he wrote about his thorn in the flesh. He said it was to prevent him from getting puffed up with pride about his visions. The apostle appealed three times to God for relief, and we assume that he would have repented of his pride. God's forgiveness is indicated by the assurance that his grace is sufficient. Still, God did not remove the thorn so that Paul might learn to depend utterly on God. Repentance and forgiveness are not about evading punishment but being embraced by God's presence.

How then should we respond to unrepentant enemies? This is what we will explore in the following two chapters.

---

30. David Toshio Tsumura, *1 Samuel*, NICOT (Grand Rapids: Eerdmans, 2007), 407.
31. Arnold, *1 & 2 Samuel*, 222.

5

What Is Vengeance and Enemy Love in the Old Testament?

Dictionary.com defines the verb "revenge" as "to exact punishment or expiation for a wrong on behalf of, especially in a resentful and vindictive spirit." On the same website, "vengeance" is "violent revenge." Little wonder that Christians believe that "revenge" and "vengeance" are unacceptable.

The more academic definitions of vengeance are toned down. Merriam-Webster Online says it is "punishment inflicted in retaliation for an injury or offense." Cambridge English Dictionary Online defines it as "the punishing of someone for harming you or your friends or family, or the wish for such punishment to happen." Its synonyms are "retribution" and "repayment."

In other words, vengeance is simply the desire for justice. Psychologists have found this to be a basic human instinct, even in young children. In a November 2020 Yale study, 251 children between the ages of four and seven were each given an iPad and shown a video of a child tearing up another youngster's artwork. The children then had to decide whether to punish the culprit by taking away his or her iPad. However, if they chose to do so, they were told that their own iPad would also be taken away.

The next step gets interesting. The children were divided into two groups, with the first group being told that if they chose to punish the wrongdoer, the culprit would lose his or her iPad without being told why. The second group were informed that if they punished the wrongdoer, that child would be told that it was for ripping up the drawing.

About a quarter of the children in the first group decided to punish the transgressor even though it meant losing their own iPads. The second group, who knew that the wrongdoers would be told why they were being disciplined, were 24 percent more likely to impose punishment than the first group.

The study's authors concluded that retribution is a driving force in young children's moral judgment. Moreover, it is not just out of a desire to make people suffer. "Children seem equipped at an early age with both a desire for [offenders] to receive their just deserts, and a desire to have them improve their behaviour for next time," said the lead author.[1]

It seems that human beings have an innate sense of justice that calls for vengeance on the offender in the hope that he or she will change. Similarly, God's vengeance serves both justice and reformation, though the unrepentant are left only with justice. In the first part of this chapter, we look at what vengeance means in the legal, prophetic, narrative, and prayer genres of the OT. Despite the emphasis on retribution, the OT also encourages love for the enemy, which will be discussed in the second half of the chapter.

Vengeance in the OT

The Hebrew root for vengeance is *naqam* and it occurs seventy-nine times in the OT. It can be used positively or negatively, depending on the context. In a few texts, it refers to a wrongful act, such as holding a grudge (Lev 19:18) and attacking the innocent (Jer 20:10; Lam 3:60), or it is used in the noun form, that is, "avenger," to describe enemies of God (Ps 8:2) and his people (Ps 44:16).[2]

However, the predominant occurrence of *naqam* is in connection with the execution of justice, which can be found in various texts: legal procedures, prophecies against Israel or Israel's enemies, historical texts, and prayers. Legal regulations include the death penalty for bloodshed (Gen 4:15, 25; Exod 21:20–21) and the husband's right against one who has committed adultery with his wife (e.g. Prov 6:34). The person taking vengeance can be God himself (Gen 4) or the legal community (Exod 21; Prov 6). *Naqam* is thus punishment for a crime. It also functions as protection for the victim, as demonstrated in Exodus 21:20: "When a slave-owner strikes a male or female slave with a rod and the slave dies immediately, the owner shall be punished [passive of *naqam*]."[3] Slave-owners are thereby warned, showing the preventive aspect of *naqam*.

---

1. Julia Marshall, Daniel A. Yudkin, and Molly J. Crockett, "Children Punish Third Parties to Satisfy Both Consequentialist and Retributive Motives," *Nature Human Behaviour* 5 (2021): 361–68, https://doi.org/10.1038/s41562-020-00975-9.

2. H. G. L. Peels, *The Vengeance of God: The Meaning of the Root NQM and the Function of the NQM-Texts in the Context of Divine Revelation in the Old Testament*, Oudtestamentische Studiën (Leiden: Brill, 1995), 61.

3. Peels, *Vengeance of God*, 79.

In prophetic texts, God takes vengeance against Israel when they break his law and rebel against his covenant (Lev 26:25; Isa 1:24; 59:17; Jer 5:9, 29; 9:9; Ezek 24:8). The background of these texts shows that God is concerned with the welfare of his people, especially the poor. He is portrayed as Judge, King, and Warrior, and he acts to preserve justice and restore the covenant. Again, *naqam* is about disciplining the wrongdoer and saving the victims.[4]

In several other prophetic texts,[5] God promises vengeance against enemy nations. This theme is prominent in Moses's Song (Deut 32:1–43), and we will pay close attention to verse 35 because Paul cites it in Romans 12. The following verses are where *naqam* is used:

> [35] Vengeance [*naqam*] is mine, and recompense,
>> for the time when their foot shall slip;
> because the day of their calamity is at hand,
>> their doom comes swiftly. . . .
> [41] when I whet my flashing sword,
>> and my hand takes hold on judgement;
> I will take vengeance [*naqam*] on my adversaries,
>> and will repay those who hate me. . . .
> [43] Praise, O nations,[6] his people,
>> worship him, all you gods!
> For he will avenge [*naqam*] the blood of his children,
>> and take vengeance [*naqam*] on his adversaries;
> he will repay those who hate him,
>> and cleanse the land for his people.

God will put an end to the scornful speech and poisonous acts of the enemy to vindicate his people (32:36):

> Indeed the LORD will vindicate [*din*] his people,
>> have compassion on his servants,
> when he sees that their power is gone,
>> neither bond nor free remaining.

Vengeance is thus related to "vindicate" (Hebrew *din*), a legal decision justifying the innocent. The Song of Moses ends in verse 43 with a summons to the

---

4. Peels, 132.

5. Isa 34:8; 35:4; 47:3; 61:2; 63:4; Jer 46:10; 50:15, 28; 51:6, 11, 36; Ezek 25:12, 14, 15, 17; Mic 5:14; Nah 1:2.

6. NRSV has "heavens," but I follow the Hebrew text in using "nations." See Peels, *Vengeance of God*, 141–44.

nations to praise God's people because God will take vengeance for them. The "vengeance of God forms the ground and content of the universal praise of God's people; without vengeance there would be no future."[7]

God's *naqam* is also demonstrated in the historical narratives.[8] H. G. L. Peels writes that such punishment is related to God keeping the covenant as a just God, whether in personal (1 Sam 24:13; 2 Sam 4:8) or national (Judg 11:36) situations.[9] Lastly, vengeance is prayed for in Psalms and Jeremiah (Pss 58:10; 79:10; 94:1; 149:7; Jer 11:20; 15:15; 20:12). In these prayers, the justice system has usually failed the victims, and so they call out for God's vengeance but refrain from taking vengeance themselves.[10]

The God of vengeance in the OT is the same God in the NT. Deuteronomy 32:35, "Vengeance is mine," is cited twice in the NT, in Romans 12:19 and Hebrews 10:30. The NT also contains curses, which echo the psalms of vengeance (e.g. Matt 21:18–21; 25:41; Acts 8:20; 13:11; Gal 1:8; 1 Cor 16:22; Rev 6:10). In the parable of the unjust judge (Luke 18:1–8), Jesus encouraged his followers to keep asking God for *ekdikeō* (vengeance).[11] At the final judgment, God will avenge (*ekdikeō*) his people (Rev 6:10; 19:2).

In the psalms of vengeance, the psalmists never curse their adversaries directly but ask God to do so. In fact, "imprecatory" psalms means cursing psalms, and to understand why this is allowed requires an explanation of the ancient Near Eastern context. Curses were employed to ensure truth in judicial procedures, force obedience in treaties, frighten off thieves, guarantee honesty in transactions, and so on. Thus, the curse functioned in many respects as a legal device.[12]

Whereas the wider ancient Near East viewed curses as having a blend of divine and magical power, the curse in Israel is attributed to God alone. Apart from his will, no curse is effected. For example, in Numbers 23:8, Balaam said, "How can I curse whom God has not cursed?," and again in Numbers 23:20, "See, I received a command to bless; he has blessed, and I cannot revoke it." John Day points to Deuteronomy 23:5 and Malachi 2:2 to show that God "in his sovereignty can transmute cursing into blessing and blessing into cursing."[13]

---

7. Peels, 146.

8. Judg 11:36; Num 31:2, 3; 1 Sam 24:13; 2 Sam 4:8; 22:48; 2 Kgs 9:7.

9. Peels, *Vengeance of God*, 264.

10. Peels, 234.

11. Peels, 244, 310–12.

12. Peels, 237–38.

13. Day, *Crying for Justice*, 44.

The OT makes a distinction between legitimate and illegitimate curses. Curses against parents and God earned the death penalty (Exod 21:17; Lev 24:11). However, Proverbs 26:2 says that an unjustified curse has no effect: "Like a sparrow in its flitting, like a swallow in its flying, an undeserved curse goes nowhere." Illegitimate curses are usually attributed to the mouths of enemies (Pss 10:7; 59:12; 62:4). In contrast, the psalmist's curse is an appeal to God to execute justice as the divine king and judge.[14]

How is vengeance reconciled with love for the enemy (enemy love)? In the next chapter, we will look more closely at the NT texts in Jesus's Sermon on the Mount and Paul's teaching in Romans 12:9-21 because they seem most at odds with the psalms of vengeance. Here, I will show that the NT's command to love the enemy is actually rooted in the OT.

Enemy Love in the OT

Enemy love is taught in the legal, wisdom, and narrative portions of the OT.

1. Legal Materials

> If you come across your enemy's ox or donkey wandering off, be sure to return it. If you see the donkey of someone who hates you fallen down under its load, do not leave it there; be sure you help them with it. (Exod 23:4–5 NIV)

Exodus 23:4–5 has been called "an embryo of the rule of enemy love."[15] This text stands out, for there is no penalty, unlike the case laws in Exodus 22:1–17.[16] While other laws are prohibitions ("do nots"), Exodus 23:4–5 requires

---

14. Peels, *Vengeance of God*, 238.

15. W. Schmauch, *Das Evangelium des Matthäus* (Göttingen, 1967), cited in John Piper, *"Love Your Enemies": Jesus' Love Command in the Synoptic Gospels and the Early Christian Paraenesis* (Cambridge: Cambridge University Press, 1980), 28. The principle is echoed in Lev 19:17–18.

16. Peter Enns, *Exodus*, NIVAC (Grand Rapids: Zondervan, 2000), 455.

positive actions towards an enemy, whether a fellow Israelite[17] or a foreigner[18] who lives among them.

2. Wisdom Literature

The following proverbs are about enemy love and vengeance:

> Do not say, "I will repay evil";
> > wait for the LORD, and he will help you. (Prov 20:22)

> Do not rejoice when your enemies fall,
> > and do not let your heart be glad when they stumble,
> or else the LORD will see it and be displeased,
> > and turn away his anger from them. (24:17–18)

> Do not say, "I will do to others as they have done to me;
> > I will pay them back for what they have done." (24:29)

> If your enemies are hungry, give them bread to eat;
> > and if they are thirsty, give them water to drink;
> for you will heap coals of fire on their heads,
> > and the LORD will reward you. (25:21–22)

Proverbs 20:22 establishes non-retaliation on the basis that God is the one who repays.[19] There is no place for taking personal vengeance extra-judicially. In Exodus 21:24, the principle of *lex talionis* (i.e. the law of retaliation or "an eye for an eye," requiring the same punishment as the offence committed) is meant to guide public justice in a court of law.[20]

Proverbs 24:17–18 warns against *Schadenfreude* (taking pleasure over another's misfortune), lest God "suspends your enemy's punishment just to deprive you of your smug glee."[21] Michael V. Fox suggests two reasons for

---

17. Contrary to Piper, "*Love Your Enemies*," 28, who argues that "enemy" (*ʾoyev*) uniformly refers to a national enemy in the Pentateuch. Rather, the meaning needs to be determined by the context; e.g. Num 35:23 describes an accidental killing of a fellow Israelite who is not an enemy. Here, Exod 20–23 is addressed to Israelites.

18. Provisions for aliens are found in Lev 19:34 and Deut 10:19. Loving a non-Israelite enemy will take longer to learn but is exemplified in the book of Jonah.

19. Michael V. Fox, *Proverbs 10–31*, AB (New Haven: Yale University Press, 2009), 673, writes that while the second parallel line has "save" rather than "repay" or "avenge," the salvation here is not the extrication of the pious person from harm but the defeat of that person's enemies as well.

20. *Lex talionis* is repeated in Lev 24:20 and Deut 19:21.

21. Fox, *Proverbs 10–31*, 750.

God's displeasure: God himself takes no sadistic delight in punishing people but desires their repentance; and rejoicing over another's downfall is a sign of arrogance, thinking that we are better than others.[22]

Proverbs 25:21–22 counsels one to meet the enemy's needs. "Coals of fire" is a crux in this text, one which is crucial for understanding Romans 12:19–20, where Paul quotes this proverb. Gordon Zerbe summarizes three interpretations: "standard," "apocalyptic," and "mediating." The standard interpretation takes "coals of fire" to be pangs of remorse that will lead to change, the apocalyptic interpretation understands the coals as divine judgment, while the mediating position incorporates both views – that is, one should love the enemy and hope for his or her conversion, but there will be judgment if the enemy does not repent.[23]

The standard view usually cites the third-century BC Egyptian penitential ritual. The wrongdoer is forced to show repentance by carrying a staff in his or her hand and a tray of burning coals on his or her head. However, there is no evidence that biblical writers knew such a late practice. Also, forced repentance seems more like an act of punishment that does not lead to reconciliation.[24]

Zerbe takes the view that the coals of fire refer to divine punishment. In the OT, live coals symbolize divine wrath (2 Sam 22:9, 13), punishment of the wicked (Ps 140:11), or an evil passion (Prov 6:28).[25] In all these references, "coals of fire" is a metaphor for harm. Furthermore, reading Proverbs 25:22 in the light of 20:22 confirms that the coals are related to retribution:[26]

> . . . for you will heap coals of fire on their heads,
> and the LORD will reward [*shalam*] you. (Prov 25:22)

> Do not say, "I will repay [*shalam*] evil";
> wait for the LORD, and he will help you. (20:22)

---

22. Fox, 750.

23. Gordon Zerbe, "Paul's Ethic of Nonretaliation and Peace," in *The Love of Enemy and Nonretaliation in the New Testament*, ed. Willard M. Swartley (Louisville: Westminster John Knox, 1992), 182–83.

24. Zerbe, "Paul's Ethic," 196.

25. Zerbe, 197; Piper, "*Love Your Enemies*," 115. Thomas R. Schreiner, *Romans*, BECNT (Grand Rapids: Baker, 1998), 675, also refers to 2 Esd (4 Ezra) 16:53: "Sinners must not say that they have not sinned; for God will burn coals of fire on the head of everyone who says, 'I have not sinned before God and his glory.'" Though 2 Esd may be post-Pauline, it shows that the metaphor was used for God's judgment.

26. Contrary to Bruce K. Waltke, *The Book of Proverbs Chapters 15–31*, NICOT (Grand Rapids: Eerdmans, 2005), 331. He adopts the standard interpretation and does not read Prov 25:22 in the light of 20:22.

In 25:22, heaping coals by helping the enemy leads to a "reward," which is the same Hebrew word for "repay" in 20:22. Thus, heaping coals is related to God's judgment for evil. Doing good adds to the enemy's punishment by showing how guilty he or she is. Like Zerbe, I adopt the mediating interpretation,[27] which will be explained in relation to Romans 12 in the next chapter.

Michael V. Fox cites an ancient Egyptian wisdom text that has much in common with the book of Proverbs. *Amenemope* 5.1–6 says,

> Steer! Let us ferry the evil man across,
>   so that we not act like him!
> Raise him up, give him your hand;
>   leave him in the hands of God.
> Fill his belly with your own bread,
>   that he be sated and ashamed.

Like Proverbs 25:21–22, *Amenemope* teaches one to do good to the enemy, trusting the deity to bring the matter to a just conclusion.[28] This approach ensures that one does not emulate the enemy's evil behaviour. Though *Amenemope* mentions the enemy's shame, there is no certainty that the enemy will change, so it would refer to the shame of suffering divine judgment. One should do good to enemies and leave vengeance to God.

3. Historical Narratives

We can see the application of the Proverbs teaching in the life of David when he declined to kill Saul though he twice had the opportunity to do so. David's reasoning is found in his speeches in 1 Samuel.

> May the LORD judge [*shaphat*] between me and you! May the LORD avenge [*naqam*] me on you; but my hand shall not be against you. As the ancient proverb says, "Out of the wicked comes forth wickedness"; but my hand shall not be against you. Against whom has the king of Israel come out? Whom do you pursue? A dead dog? A single flea? May the LORD therefore be judge [*dayyan*], and give sentence [*shaphat*] between me and you. May he see to it, and plead my cause [*riv*], and vindicate [*shaphat*] me against you. (1 Sam 24:12–15)

---

27. Zerbe, "Paul's Ethic," 201.
28. Fox, *Proverbs 10–31*, 788.

David appealed to God as the judge and prayed for the LORD to execute vengeance (*naqam*) for him. The verb "judge" (*shaphat*) is used three times in 24:12, 15. Together with other words like "cause" (*riv*) and "judge" (*dayyan*) in 25:15, it sets God's vengeance in a judicial context. "It is not the thirst for blood but the thirst for justice that is the ruling motif."[29]

> David said, "As the LORD lives, the LORD will strike him down; or his day will come to die; or he will go down into battle and perish. The LORD forbid that I should raise my hand against the LORD's anointed; but now take the spear that is at his head, and the water-jar, and let us go. (1 Sam 26:10–11)

In this second incident, David refused to let his soldier kill Saul, but left Saul's fate to God. He speaks with an oath of certainty ("as the LORD lives") that God will strike his enemy. Thus, David could practise enemy love precisely because he trusted in God's vengeance. David's speeches upon sparing Saul also show that loving the enemy includes reasoning with or correcting the enemy as well as defending one's innocence.

In the next chapter, we will look at the NT's development of the OT ideas of vengeance and enemy love.

---

29. Peels, *Vengeance of God*, 256.

6

What is Enemy Love and Vengeance in the New Testament?

In the OT, enemy love goes together with divine vengeance. How does this square with Jesus's and Paul's commands to love one's enemies? In this chapter, we will look closely at the following texts:

- Jesus's Sermon on the Mount
- Paul's Epistle to the Romans
- Relevant texts in 1 Corinthians, 1 Thessalonians, and 1 Peter

Jesus's Sermon on the Mount (Matt 5:38–48)
1. Lex Talionis

> [38] You have heard that it was said, "Eye for eye, and tooth for tooth."
> [39] But I tell you, do not resist an evil person. If anyone slaps you on the right cheek, turn to them the other cheek also. [40] And if anyone wants to sue you and take your shirt, hand over your coat as well. [41] If anyone forces you to go one mile, go with them two miles. [42] Give to the one who asks you, and do not turn away from the one who wants to borrow from you. (NIV)

Matthew 5:39, "do not resist an evil person," has been taken to mean either non-retaliation or non-resistance. Non-resistance means passively accepting abuse, while non-retaliation allows the victim to defend him- or herself. I believe that Jesus is speaking about *non-retaliation*, together with radical acts of love for the enemy. This reading will be clear from three aspects: (1) the application of *lex talionis*, (2) the meaning of "resist" (from the Greek root *anthistēmi*), and (3) the examples of non-retaliation.

First, the OT law of *lex talionis* (Exod 21:24; Lev 24:20; Deut 19:21) was applied in the courts to limit personal vengeance. It was a legal principle rather than one that was carried out literally, since the law allowed other forms of compensation (Exod 21:26; Lev 24:18).[1] John Piper takes the extreme position that Jesus was doing away with this OT norm because it was a concession to people's hardness of heart.[2] However, this would undermine a fundamental principle of justice, which God himself applies (see Rom 12 below). Rather, Jesus was not abolishing the Torah but correcting its abuse. For example, he did not do away with the laws of murder and adultery but expanded their application to inward thoughts. Thus, Jesus was not negating the application of *lex talionis* in a legal case but prohibiting its extension to personal vengeance.[3]

The second issue is the meaning of do not "resist" (*anthistēmi*) in verse 39. The English translation implies a passive stance, but it is used both passively and actively in the NT. When understood in the active sense, Jesus is prohibiting actions against the offender. For example, in Acts 13:8, Elymas the magician resisted (*anthistēmi*) Paul by trying to turn the proconsul away from the faith.[4] Additionally, in the Greek version of the OT, *anthistēmi* is often used in a legal context. Deuteronomy 19:18 is especially relevant where the rule of *lex talionis* is applied to a malicious witness who gives false testimony "in opposition" (*anthistēmi*) against another.[5] Thus, to resist is to act or speak to the detriment of another. What Jesus forbids is not defensive actions but vengeful retaliation.

---

1. G. J. Wenham, *The Book of Leviticus*, NICOT (Grand Rapids: Eerdmans, 1979), 312. Only in the case of premeditated murder was such compensation forbidden (Num 35:31).

2. Piper, *"Love Your Enemies,"* 89, uses Moses's law of divorce as an example of making a concession to the human hardness of heart (Mark 10:2–9). However, *lex talionis* is a principle of justice, not a concession.

3. Hagner, *Matthew 1–13*, 130; France, *Matthew*, 218; Michael J. Wilkins, *Matthew*, NIVAC (Grand Rapids: Zondervan, 2004), 249.

4. Other examples in the NT: in Gal 2:11, Paul said that he resisted Cephas because the latter would not fellowship with Gentiles; 2 Tim 3:8 compares false teachers who resisted the truth to the Egyptian magicians who resisted Moses.

5. Blomberg, *Matthew*, 113; e.g. Isa 50:8. So also Richard A. Horsley, "Ethics and Exegesis: 'Love Your Enemies' and the Doctrine of Nonviolence," in Swartley, *Love of Enemy and Nonretaliation*, 82. In contrast, France, *Matthew*, 219, disagrees with the legal meaning and takes a non-resistance view. While Dorothy Jean Weaver, "Transforming Nonresistance: From *Lex Talionis* to 'Do Not Resist the Evil One,'" in Swartley, *Love of Enemy and Nonretaliation*, 41, recognizes the legal use in the OT, she takes a non-resistant view because she does not consider the context in Matt 5:38–42.

Third, the examples given by Jesus are about non-retaliation rather than acceptance of abuse. Slapping someone on the right cheek means that the offender used the back of his or her right hand to hit the victim, which is not so much a physical attack but a shameful insult.[6] Walter Wink explains that in the Jewish context, the left hand was used only for unclean tasks, so offering the left cheek would be inviting the wrongdoer to act with the back of the left hand, rendering him- or herself unclean. Alternatively, the abuser would have to strike the offered left cheek with the fist of his or her right hand, which would acknowledge the victim as an equal.[7] Thus, turning the left cheek is to take a defensive stance against humiliation.[8] Christians are certainly not called to be doormats.

In the rest of the examples, Jesus expands non-retaliation to doing good beyond the legal requirements. Exodus 22:25–27 and Deuteronomy 24:12–13 state that the creditor must return a cloak taken as a pledge by sunset, but a disciple is encouraged to be generous when repaying a loan. The third example shows that a disciple is to treat a Gentile enemy in the same way. A Roman soldier had the right to enlist a member of the subject population to carry his equipment for a mile, but a disciple is to go an extra mile.[9] The final charge in verse 42 to give or lend to anyone encourages generosity over legalism. In the following segment on enemy love, Jesus lays out the theological basis for his radical teaching.

2. Enemy Love

[43] You have heard that it was said, "Love your neighbour and hate your enemy." [44] But I tell you, love your enemies and pray for those

---

6. Nolland, *Matthew*, 258, n. 235, cites a rabbinic law that a slap with the back of the hand calls for twice the payment in recompense.

7. Walter Wink, "Neither Passivity Nor Violence: Jesus' Third Way (Matt. 5:38–42 par.)," in Swartley, *Love of Enemy and Nonretaliation*, 104–5, cites Qumran to show that even gesturing with the left hand carried the penalty of ten days' penance.

8. I disagree with France, *Matthew*, 220, who because of his view on non-resistance writes that one can stand up for a principle or for others but not for oneself when under threat. Clearly, Paul defended himself in Acts 16:37; 22:25; 25:9–12. In a conflict with a fellow disciple, one should follow the procedures in Matt 18:15–17.

9. Wink, "Jesus' Third Way," 106–11, argues that handing over one's undergarment would shame the creditor and going the second mile could cause trouble for the Roman soldier who had to follow the strict requirement of the law that allowed only one mile. Thus, Wink writes that Jesus was teaching defiance in the context of a social struggle. However, to interpret Jesus's motivation as instigating defiance goes against the Sermon on the Mount in which the Lord counselled love for the enemy.

who persecute you, [45] that you may be children of your Father in heaven. He causes his sun to rise on the evil and the good, and sends rain on the righteous and the unrighteous. [46] If you love those who love you, what reward will you get? Are not even the tax collectors doing that? [47] And if you greet only your own people, what are you doing more than others? Do not even pagans do that? [48] Be perfect, therefore, as your heavenly Father is perfect. (Matthew 5:43–48, NIV)

The basis for enemy love is not transactional reciprocity but to be like God, our heavenly Father. The saying "Love your neighbour" is from Leviticus 19:18, but the second part, "Hate your enemy," is questionable. Two issues need to be considered: (1) What does hatred of enemies mean in the OT? and (2) What do love and prayer for enemies entail?

First, some OT texts that seem to promote hatred against enemies are not about personal animosity but a concern for God's holiness. For example, there are several Deuteronomic texts against foreigners, such as Deuteronomy 20:17–18:

You shall annihilate them – the Hittites and the Amorites, the Canaanites and the Perizzites, the Hivites and the Jebusites – just as the LORD your God has commanded, so that they may not teach you to do all the abhorrent things that they do for their gods, and you thus sin against the LORD your God.

The reason for eliminating the enemies is to protect God's people from idolatry. Exceptions like Rahab and Ruth, who chose to worship Israel's God, proved that religious rather than ethnic affiliation determined acceptance. Similarly, Psalm 139:19–22 speaks of hating those who hate the LORD because that would mean detesting wickedness.[10]

Admittedly, OT texts that promote goodwill to personal enemies generally refer to fellow Israelites or "well-disposed foreigners" (Lev 19:34; Deut 10:19) who were living among them.[11] However, the Jews in Jesus's time drew a legalistic implication that one could hate one's enemies for any reason. And, it was not just pagans who could be hated, but also those who did not love

---

10. D. A. Carson, *Love in Hard Places* (Wheaton: Crossway, 2002), 41, cites 2 Chr 19:2 as another example: "Jehu son of Hanani the seer went out to meet him and said to King Jehoshaphat, 'Should you help the wicked and love those who hate the LORD? Because of this, wrath has gone out against you from the LORD.'" The king is told that he should not make alliances to promote the agendas of those who are against God.

11. France, *Matthew*, 225.

you (Matt 5:46–47). Just as *lex talionis* was distorted for personal vengeance, so love for neighbours was perverted to justify hate for personal enemies.[12] On the contrary, Jesus taught that one should love others irrespective of race and religion (the Gentiles), social status (tax collectors), or even morality (persecutors, the evil and unrighteous).

Second, what then does love for the enemy entail? Carson recounts a prayer meeting held a few days after the 11 September 2001 attacks on the USA which destroyed the twin towers of the World Trade Center in New York City. A woman prayed, "Lord, bless Osama bin Laden. Pour out your blessing upon him. You have commanded us to pray for our enemies, and so we pray that you will bless him." Carson asked whether this was the right thing to pray.[13]

Such a prayer misreads Jesus's intent in his sermon, which was to correct hatred and prejudice, not to prosper an evildoer. It misunderstands the meaning of "bless," which is to call on the life-giving power of God for another, and that must include repentance for sin in the first place. More broadly, it overlooks the context of Jesus's sermon, which includes fiery judgment on those who are murderously angry (5:21–22), hypocrites (6:2, 5, 16), false prophets (7:19), and evildoers (7:23). As France puts it, "His concept of love is apparently not at the level of simply being nice to people and of allowing error to go unchallenged. Love is not incompatible with controversy and rebuke."[14]

Loving enemies means providing for what they need, like God's providential gifts of sun and rain, but there is no command to forgive enemies. Love is not incompatible with God's vengeance, and Paul makes this clear in Romans 12.

Paul in Romans 12:9–21
One Another Section

> [9] Let love be genuine. Abhor what is evil; hold fast to what is good.
> [10] Love **one another** with brotherly affection. Outdo *one another* in showing honour.
> [11] Do not be slothful in zeal, be fervent in spirit, serve the Lord.

---

12. Carson, *Love in Hard Places*, 44.

13. Carson, 108.

14. France, *Matthew*, 226. The Lucan parallel of Jesus's sermon adds a unique socio-economic emphasis: enemy love is primarily to help the needy, even if they are your enemies. Luke took Matt 5:42, "Do not refuse anyone who wants to borrow from you," a step further by saying, "If anyone takes away your goods, do not ask for them again" (Luke 6:30) – i.e. after lending, the disciples were not even to ask for their loan back.

¹² Rejoice in hope, be patient in tribulation, be constant in prayer.
¹³ Contribute to the needs of the saints and seek to show [diōkō] hospitality.
¹⁴ Bless those who persecute [diōkō] you; bless and do not curse them.
¹⁵ Rejoice with those who rejoice, weep with those who weep.
¹⁶ Live in harmony with **one another**. Do not be haughty, but associate with the lowly. Never be wise in your own sight. (ESV)

Dealing with Evil Section

¹⁷ **Repay no one evil [kakos] for evil [kakos],**
but give thought to do what is honourable in the sight of *all*.
¹⁸ If possible, so far as it depends on you, live peaceably with *all*.
¹⁹ Beloved, never avenge yourselves, but leave it to the wrath of God,
for [gar] it is written, "Vengeance is mine, I will repay, says the Lord."
²⁰ To the contrary, "if your enemy is hungry, feed him;
if he is thirsty, give him something to drink;
for [gar] by so doing you will heap burning coals on his head."
²¹ **Do not be overcome by evil [kakos], but overcome evil [kakos] with good.** (ESV)

This text raises a few questions: (1) While persecutors of the church especially need to be shown love and will face judgment if they remain unrepentant, does vengeance apply to all enemies outside and inside the church? (2) What does "burning coals" refer to? (3) How is leaving vengeance to God consistent with blessing and not cursing the enemy?

First, who are the enemies? Zerbe argues that Paul was referring to the church's persecutors (12:14) based on the Greek word *diōkō*, which Paul used for hostile outsiders.¹⁵ While this is correct, I disagree with Zerbe when he concludes that the teaching about vengeance applies to the church's enemies

---

15. Zerbe, "Paul's Ethic," 186.

rather than church members. Most commentators see 12:14–21 as another section dealing with those persecuting the church.

However, this would make verse 16 about living in internal harmony with "one another" out of place. Instead, I propose that verses 9–16 focus on church relationships, indicated by the *inclusio* of "one another" in verses 10 and 16 (shown in bold in the above quotation of the passage). Verses 17–21 then deal with enemies, enveloped by the double reference to evil (*kakos*) in verses 17 and 21 (also shown in bold). In this section, Christians are to live peaceably with "all" (vv. 17–18), that is, both those inside and outside the church.[16] Thus, verses 9–15 give instructions on how to live in harmony with one another, while verses 17–21 deal with disharmonious people in general.

Furthermore, Paul is believed to be paraphrasing four "sayings" of Jesus in 12:14, 17, 19–20, and 21.[17] Verse 14 can be compared to Matthew 5:44, "Love your enemies and pray for those who persecute [*diōkontas*] you," and Luke 6:27–28, "But I say to you that listen, Love your enemies, do good to those who hate you, bless those who curse you, pray for those who abuse you." In his Sermon on the Mount, Jesus taught his disciples not to resist those who insulted them, took their tunics, or forced them to go the second mile – offences committed by Jewish insiders and Roman outsiders. In other words, Romans 12:17–21 applies to both fellow disciples and persecutors. Thus, to live peaceably with all (12:18) in the larger perspective would involve not just enduring a wrong but also mediation in the church (Matt 18:15–17; 1 Cor 6:1–6). When the other party (whether Christian or non-Christian) is unrepentant, then one is to leave vengeance to God.

Now we come to the second question of the burning coals. Romans 12:19 and 20 show a parallel structure, with each providing a basis for the commands beginning with "for" (*gar*). This repetition would make "burning coals" synonymous with "vengeance":

> Rom 12:19: for [*gar*] it is written, "Vengeance is mine, I will repay, says the Lord."

---

16. Verse 14 about persecutors simply continues the rhetoric in v. 13 by pairing a positive command with a negative one, both of which play on the word *diōkō*: one is to pursue (*diōkontes*) hospitality and not curse those who pursue you (*diōkontas*). Schreiner, *Romans*, 663, makes the same paragraph division without explaining the rationale for v. 14.

17. Richard N. Longenecker, *The Epistle to the Romans*, NIGTC (Grand Rapids: Eerdmans, 2016), 939, explains that these references are indicated by the imperatives ("bless," "repay," "give," "feed," "give drink," "overcome"), which stand apart from the absolute participles used in the rest of this segment. However, Robert Jewett, *Romans*, Hermeneia (Minneapolis: Augsburg Fortress, 2006), 771, shows that the command in 12:17 is closer to the OT pseudepigraphical work Jos. Asen. 28:14, "Do not pay back evil for evil to any person."

Rom 12:20: for [*gar*] by so doing you will heap burning coals on his head. (ESV)

This interpretation is consistent with our conclusion in the previous chapter, that coals in Proverbs 25:22 refer to God's judgment rather than pangs of remorse that lead to repentance. Is such punishment an eschatological or a historical promise? That is, do we wait for the final judgment or expect the punishment in this life? Zerbe joins Piper in taking the apocalyptic view, based on Paul's use of "fire" as referring to the final judgment (1 Cor 3:13, 15; 2 Thess 1:8).[18]

On the other hand, James D. G. Dunn, in his commentary, recognizes that the divine wrath in 12:19 may not necessarily refer to a future judgment.[19] Indeed, Paul also wrote about the revelation of God's present wrath (Rom 1:18) and the execution of his wrath by human authorities (Rom 13:4–5). Additionally, Romans 12:21 calls on Christians to overcome evil with good. While the final triumph may take place in the eschaton, the imperative implies that victory is possible in the present.

The OT envisages both present and future vengeance. Proverbs 25:22 with its reference to the burning coals belongs to the wisdom genre, which is concerned with consequences observed in life. It has been mentioned that Romans 12:19 quotes from Moses's Song in Deuteronomy 32:35, "Vengeance is mine, I will repay, says the Lord," and God so acted against Israel's enemies in history. Such retribution is pushed into a future "day of the Lord" (e.g. Isa 61:2; Joel 3:14) in the later exilic and post-exilic writings. Thus, divine punishment is both historical and eschatological. When Jesus warned Israel about the coming judgment, he referred both to the 70 AD destruction of Jerusalem and the final judgment (Mark 13//Matt 24).

With coals referring to divine punishment, the third question is how is vengeance compatible with blessing and not cursing enemies (Rom 12:14)? To bless involves meeting the enemies' needs, but its fundamental sense is to pray God's gracious power on someone. Early Jewish texts showed that these included prayers for leniency, repentance, or salvation.[20] We are to bless out of

---

18. Zerbe, "Paul's Ethic," 197, although he admits that the references are not many. Also Piper, "*Love Your Enemies,*" 115.

19. James D. G. Dunn, *Romans 9–16*, WBC (Dallas: Word, 1988), 749.

20. Zerbe, "Paul's Ethic," 189, n. 84, lists prayer that God not hold abusing brothers accountable (T. Jos. 18:2; T. Benj. 3:6–7) and prayer for abusers' repentance instead of cursing them (b. Ber. 10a, attributed to R. Meir).

love (Rom 12:9), with the hope that the persecutor will change but regardless of whether he or she does.

If the wrongdoer does not repent, one is to hand him or her over to God's vengeance (Rom 12:20). Seeking retribution is not the "cursing" prohibited in 12:14. Since Paul is echoing Luke 6:28, which uses "curse" synonymously with "abuse," then the Christian is not to return insult with insult. Instead, Zerbe says that "the believer prays for the best possible fate of the abuser but leaves the final realisation of justice to God."[21] Thus, we are not called to forgive unrepentant enemies but to love them. Love and vengeance go hand in hand as a reflection of God's grace and holiness.

Other Texts on Enemy Love

Some other epistles seem to promote non-resistance in the name of enemy love. However, when these passages are read in their contexts, enemy love does not equate to passive acceptance of a wrong, but may call for self-defence, discipline, or trusting in God's vengeance.

> When reviled, we bless; when persecuted, we endure; when slandered, we speak kindly [parakaleō]. (1 Cor 4:12–13)

In 1 Corinthians, Paul writes to defend his apostleship, which shows that non-retaliation does not mean a passive acceptance of what is wrong, especially when dealing with an internal church problem. In fact, "speak kindly" in verse 13 is from the Greek parakaleō, which Gordon Fee suggests is better translated as "humbly make an appeal," as Paul does in this epistle.[22]

> In fact, to have lawsuits at all with one another is already a defeat for you. Why not rather be wronged? Why not rather be defrauded? (1 Cor 6:7)

When this passage is read in context, Paul is not saying that one should acquiesce in a wrong. Rather, he is shaming the rival parties by saying that it is better to be wronged and defrauded than to sue each other in a secular court. What the apostle advised them to do was to find a wise mediator in the

---

21. Zerbe, "Paul's Ethic," 200. Piper, "Love Your Enemies," 118–19, writes that God's judgment frees the Christian from "the insidious tendency in every man to keep an account of wrongs (1 Cor 13:6) in the name of justice." However, it is not wrong to seek justice as long as it is entrusted to God.

22. Gordon Fee, The First Epistle to the Corinthians, NICNT (Grand Rapids: Eerdmans, 1987), 180.

church (1 Cor 6:5), consistent with Matthew 18:15–20. In fact, he assures the one wronged that God will be the ultimate judge (1 Cor 6:9).

> See that none of you repays evil for evil, but always seek to do good to one another and to all. (1 Thess 5:15)

Like the teaching in 1 Corinthians 6, this verse occurs in a context of instructions to the church community. Non-retaliation includes correction, as stated in the preceding verse: "admonish the idlers" (1 Thess 5:14). Idleness continued to be a problem in the Thessalonian church, so Paul called for more stringent discipline in 2 Thessalonians 3:10: "Anyone unwilling to work should not eat." The apostle believed that tough love is part of doing good.

> When he was abused, he did not return abuse; when he suffered, he did not threaten; but he entrusted [*paredidou*] himself to the one who judges justly [*krinonti dikaiōs*]. (1 Pet 2:23)

The word "entrusted" (*paredidou*) is in the Greek indicative imperfect tense, expressing ongoing activity that characterized Jesus's life and ministry. The verb has no object in this verse (though the English translation supplies "himself"), meaning that Jesus kept handing over to God every dimension of his life, including the fate of his enemies. Thus, Thomas R. Schreiner says that we are not to be stoics in suffering and merely put on a brave face, but know that "believers triumph over evil, because they trust that God will vindicate them and judge their enemies."[23]

> Do not repay evil for evil or abuse for abuse; but, on the contrary, repay with a blessing. It is for this that you were called – that you might inherit a blessing. . . .
> For the eyes of the Lord are on the righteous,
> and his ears are open to their prayer.
> But the face of the Lord is against those who do evil. (1 Pet 3:9, 12)

Commentators note that in the ancient world, people demonstrated their innocence by arguing passionately against their accusers, so Peter's exhortation was revolutionary.[24] In the above passage, Paul advised slaves who were

---

23. Thomas R. Schreiner, *1, 2 Peter, Jude*, NAC (Nashville: Broadman & Holman, 2003), 133. John H. Elliot, *1 Peter*, AB (New York: Doubleday, 2000), 547–50, notes that 1 Pet 2:21–25 echoes the suffering servant of Isa 53. Schreiner, *1, 2 Peter, Jude*, 144, also sees an allusion to Jer 11:18–23, where the prophet describes himself as a gentle lamb led to the slaughter while trusting in God's judgment. For Jeremiah's persecutors, the judgment eventually took place with Jerusalem's destruction in 586 BC.

24. Schreiner, 143; Elliot, *1 Peter*, 607.

harshly treated by their masters to follow Jesus's example of non-retaliation and entrusting judgment to God (2:18–23). Like Romans 12:19, the promise of retribution in 1 Peter 3:12 shows that the hope of divine vengeance enables one to return good for evil.

Conclusion

In the book *Suing for Peace: A Guide for Resolving Life's Conflicts*,[25] psychiatry lecturer and lawyer James Kimmel argues that in the American adversarial context, the more a party seeks justice, the more bitter he or she becomes. One can become addicted to outrage. He advocates that instead of seeking justice against enemies, one should practise "non-justice." Kimmel explains his "non-justice" model in which the abused goes through a process of imagining him- or herself as playing the role of the prosecutor, victim, defendant, defence lawyer, judge, and even the prison warden carrying out the sentence. The purpose is to enable the sufferer to take control of his or her pain and satisfy his or her desire for justice.[26]

In a casual experiment, a reporter took an angry political activist through the above exercise and asked whether he felt better. Unfortunately, the person said, "No." The impromptu experiment may have been flawed because it was not carried out thoroughly. Kimmel's method may provide some psychological relief, but it still leaves open the vexing question of whether justice is possible.

Only when we know that God is the ultimate judge can we relinquish our anger. Enemy love is possible when we entrust vengeance to God. How are we to do so? The imprecatory psalms show us the way. However, due to their vitriolic tone, many Christians are uncomfortable with these psalms. Theologians have suggested various ways to interpret them, which the next chapter will review.

---

25. James P. Kimmel, Jr., *Suing for Peace: A Guide for Resolving Life's Conflicts* (Charlottesville: Hampton Roads, 2004).

26. James Kimmel Jr., "The Nonjustice System (Miracle Court)," accessed 21 June 2021, http://nebula.wsimg.com/20d34a01f1e4845b0632d3f60c8e724a?AccessKeyId=1C256BB45AC 7AC6816BF&disposition=0&alloworigin=1.

7

Can We Pray the Psalms of Vengeance?

Can a Christian pray the psalms of vengeance?

"No," said John Wesley – at least, not the imprecatory parts of the psalms. Modern hymnals also censor the violent verses.[1] There is no agreed number of imprecatory psalms, as the curses in the lament psalms vary in intensity. The most commonly recognized ones are Psalms 35, 55, 58, 59, 69, 83, 109, 137. Christians are averse to cursing, though we have learned thus far that a curse is simply asking God for justice. So, can Christians pray these fierce psalms?

Nicholas got mad whenever his father told him to forgive his tennis coach. The coach had eliminated him from the school team because of an obscure rule which had not been made known to the participants before the games. The teenager appealed to the teacher-in-charge, but she didn't stand up for him. He was left feeling betrayed, defenceless, and depressed.

One night, Nicholas's father, who was attending my class on the Psalms of Lament at that time, decided to read Psalm 143 with him. It was a psalm that we had just studied. Nicholas shared what happened after that in his own words:

> I was fuming with my coach and teacher and yearned for revenge
> like it was an extension of my righteousness; I wanted justice. Then
> when my father and I read Psalm 143 out loud from beginning to
> end, I was encouraged by every verse – but the last one was special
> because it made me feel powerful, just when I felt powerless:

---

1. Ernest Lucas, *Exploring the Old Testament*, Vol. 3: *The Psalms and Wisdom Literature* (London: SPCK, 2004), 60.

"In your steadfast love cut off my enemies,
	and destroy all my adversaries, for I am your servant."
	(Ps 143:12)

This is the most empowering verse of the chapter. I wrote it on my wall and repeated it in my head. It carried me through the rest of my school year.

But as I read it again a year later, it humbled me. Ironically, I found comfort in realizing that I was powerless to face my enemies and change what had happened. I was comforted, knowing that I need not fight my enemies any more but leave it to God. Because of this verse, I knew my first step was to acknowledge that I should not and cannot exact justice. The second was to leave the judgment to God, knowing that he will carry out what is truly just and righteous. Now I look forward to forgiving my enemies.

(The last line was said because the teacher-in-charge had apologized to Nicholas's parents a year later due to a series of events.)

Praying the psalms of vengeance can be spiritually and emotionally healing. However, do we pray them simply because they are therapeutic, or because doing so has a theological basis? This chapter will discuss seven models of interpretation: the first five will be shown to be inadequate, but the last two will guide us in understanding them theologically and applying them spiritually. The categories below are not mutually exclusive in that the same scholar may use more than one approach.[2] The seven models are to take the imprecatory psalms as

1. Allegories

2. Human expressions

3. Socio-historical usage

4. Pre-Christian understanding

5. Messianic/prophetic declarations

6. Based on OT theologies

7. Prayers of dependence

---

2. I adapt and critique the fourteen categories of interpretation from Daniel Michael Nehrbass, *Praying Curses: The Therapeutic and Preaching Value of the Imprecatory Psalms* (Eugene: Pickwick, 2013), 13–39.

1. The Allegorical Interpretation

This approach takes the enemy as an abstract entity – that is, evil in general or the devil himself. For example, Augustine interpreted crushing the teeth in the enemies' mouths in Psalm 58 as an allegory of Jesus verbally crushing those who sought to trap him by their questions. As for dashing Babylonian infants against the rocks in Psalm 137, C. H. Spurgeon wrote that it referred to spiritual Babylon with its love for riches and power.[3] C. S. Lewis considered these "babies" on a more personal level as the small beginnings of indulgences and resentments, advising us to "knock the little bastards' brains out."[4]

However, the psalms are clearly referring to specific human enemies – Cush the Benjamite, Edom and the Ishmaelites, Moab and the Haarites, Gebal, Ammon, Amalek, Philistia, Tyre, Assyria, and so on (Pss 7:1; 83:6–8). In the NT, Jesus pronounced woes on the Pharisees, and Paul asked God to pay back the coppersmith for what he had done. As Daniel Nehrbass points out, we experience evil through human enemies, whether bullies in school or the workplace.[5]

2. Human Expressions

Another way of handling the problem is to attribute the curses to the psalmist and not the Spirit, just as not every word recorded in the Bible represents God's truth – such as words uttered by enemies and false prophets. Lewis blamed such hatred on Jewish pride against Gentiles and described the psalms as petty and vulgar: "The hatred is there – festering, gloating, undisguised – and also we should be wicked if we in any way condoned or approved it, or (worse still) used it to justify similar passions in ourselves."[6]

However, there are no signposts to distinguish human expression from the Spirit's inspiration. In a narrative, the background allows one to evaluate the speech, but the psalms are more ambiguous, unless it is clear in the context that the words of others are being referenced. An example of such a citation is Psalm 13:4: "and my enemy will say, 'I have prevailed'; my foes will rejoice because I am shaken." However, in most places, they are clearly the words of the psalmist himself, such as rejoicing over the bashing of Babylonian babies.

---

3. C. H. Spurgeon, *Treasury of David* (Grand Rapids: Baker, 1977), 188.

4. C. S. Lewis, *Reflections on the Psalms* (London: Geoffrey Bles, 1958), 136.

5. Nerhbass, *Praying Curses*, 14.

6. Lewis, *Reflections on the Psalms*, 21.

More fundamentally, the psalms are part of Israel's worship, so if imprecations are to be discouraged, then they are setting a bad example.

3. The Socio-historical Interpretation

This interpretation argues that the psalmist merely reflected his social environment in the ancient Near Eastern context, where cursing enemies was socially acceptable. Some scholars believe that curses were used like magic spells – that is, they effected change simply by their recitation. Sigmund Mowinckel writes,

> A prayer like the one in 83.10ff with its elaborate description of the disaster imprecated on the enemies of the people is evidently connected with the ancient cursing formulas, such as seers and other "divine men" and possessors of the effectual word would use against the enemy before the battle; with such words Balak expected Balaam to slay the Israelites for him.[7]

The problem with this view is that magic, sorcery, and consulting mediums were strictly forbidden in the OT on pain of death (Lev 20:27). From the Balaam account, the Israelites would have understood that a curse depends on divine and not human power because that Gentile seer could only curse or bless as permitted by God.

4. The Pre-Christian Interpretation

Some scholars consider the imprecatory psalms less enlightened and less ethical than the NT. Spurgeon took this view when he wrote, "The desire for righteous retribution is rather the spirit of the law than of the gospel."[8] More recently, Derek Kidner stated,

> It is not open to us simply to occupy the ground on which [the psalmists] stood. Between our day and theirs, our calling and theirs, stands the cross. We are ministers of reconciliation, and this is a day of good tidings. To the question, Can a Christian

---

7. Sigmund Mowinckel, *The Psalms in Israel's Worship*, Vol. 2 (Nashville: Abingdon, 1962), 29.

8. Spurgeon, *Treasury of David*, 188.

use these cries for vengeance as his own? the short answer must surely be No.[9]

The above view drives a theological wedge between the NT and the OT, which was what the second-century heretic Marcion did. He rejected the OT because he thought that the Jewish God of wrath was incompatible with the NT God of grace. This would result in a subjective understanding of the Scriptures, throwing out whatever we are uncomfortable with. In fact, enemy love originated in the OT, as discussed in chapter 5. Furthermore, such bias leads to an anti-Semitic attitude, presuming the superiority of Christians.[10]

The NT itself contains imprecations: besides Jesus's pronouncing woes on the Pharisees, Acts 1:20 applies curses from Psalms 69 and 109 to Judas, who betrayed Jesus.[11] It is usually assumed that the NT teaches us to hate the sin but love the sinner, but Jesus's many parables show that the wicked will face God's judgment in the end. Instead, as John Day says, "Love the sinner but hate the sinner."[12] Rightly hating the sinner means to seek justice with the love and hope that he or she will repent. Thus, it is when a sinner is rightly hated that he or she is rightly loved.

5. The Messianic/Prophetic Interpretation

Instead of assigning curses to imperfect humans, this approach takes them as the words of the perfect Christ. An example is at the crucifixion when Jesus cried from Psalm 22:1, "My God, my God, why have you forsaken me?" Martin Luther usually read the Psalms through a Christological lens, taking the psalmist's enemies as Jesus's Jewish persecutors.[13] James Adam is a leading modern proponent of this interpretation, arguing that only God can pray the imprecatory psalms because he is more just and holy than us.[14] Dietrich

---

9. Derek Kidner, *Psalms 1–72*, TOTC (Downers Grove: InterVarsity Press, 1975), 31–2.

10. Nehrbass, *Praying Curses*, 29.

11. Acts 1:20, "For it is written in the book of Psalms, 'Let his homestead become desolate, and let there be no one to live in it'; and 'Let another take his position of overseer.'" While Peter in Acts 1:16–22 was not cursing Judas directly, the NT believers did not have a problem with following up on the OT imprecations by finding a replacement for Judas. Though Judas had already died, they affirmed the curse's effect on his legacy.

12. Day, *Crying for Justice*, 28.

13. Nehrbass, *Praying Curses*, 42.

14. James E. Adams, *War Psalms of the Prince of Peace: Lessons from the Imprecatory Psalms* (Phillipsburg: Presbyterian & Reformed, 1991), 20, 32.

Bonhoeffer added a theological twist by regarding God's wrath as eventually falling on Christ himself, not the enemies or ourselves.[15]

The problem with the Christological interpretation is that not every part of a psalm, even if about a messiah, applies to Jesus. For instance, Psalm 69:9, "Zeal for your house will consume me," is used in John 2:17 to describe Jesus, but verse 5 of the same psalm is a confession of sin: "O God, you know my folly; the wrongs I have done are not hidden from you." The messianic psalms were historically about the Davidic king, although their expectations were ultimately fulfilled by Christ alone. Thus, the imprecatory parts cannot be taken as said only by Jesus but could be prayed by the Israelite king or community.

Some scholars simply regard the curses as OT prophecies of judgment against evildoers, either in their lifetime or on the final Day of Judgment. John Calvin took this view regarding Psalm 137:9, writing, "This is not the language of imprecation, but of prophecy, and predicts the horrors which would accompany the taking and sacking of the city of Babylon, and amongst these the atrocious cruelty of 'dashing the children against the stones.'"[16] However, even if taken as a prophecy, it does not avoid the problem of hatred for the enemies. For example, in Psalm 58:10, the psalmist rejoices in vengeance and looks forward to when the righteous will "bathe their feet in the blood of the wicked."[17]

Another issue is that not all imprecations are statements about the future. In Hebrew grammar, an imprecation may use either an imperfect verb or an imperative. The imperfect can be translated either as a wish ("may you") or as a future tense ("you will"). However, the imperative would have to be a request and not a prediction. Psalm 35:24–26, for instance, begins with the imperative, "Vindicate me, O LORD," followed by a series of imperfect verbs about the enemies being put to shame. In Hebrew syntax, the imperfects would follow the tone of the imperative and thus are requests, not an oracle about the future.[18] This understanding is reflected in the English translations:

---

15. Dietrich Bonhoeffer, *Psalms: The Prayer Book of the Bible* (Minneapolis: Augsburg, 1970), 60. However, Bonhoeffer's view that Christ took the retribution for all sinful humanity does not square with the saints' prayer for vengeance at the eschatological judgment (Rom 12:9; Rev 6:10). So also Day, *Crying for Justice*, 34.

16. John Calvin, *Commentary on the Book of Psalms*, Vol. 5 (Edinburgh: Calvin Translation Society, 1849), 194–95.

17. Nehrbass, *Praying Curses*, 39.

18. So also J. Carl Laney, "A Fresh Look at the Imprecatory Psalms," *Bibliotheca Sacra* (1981): 40.

> Vindicate me [imperative], O LORD, my God,
>   according to your righteousness,
>   and do not let them rejoice [imperfect] over me.
> Do not let them say [imperfect] to themselves,
>   "Aha, we have our heart's desire."
> Do not let them say [imperfect], "We have swallowed you up."
> Let all those who rejoice at my calamity
>   be put to shame and confusion [imperfect];
> let those who exalt themselves against me
>   be clothed with shame and dishonour [imperfect].
> (Ps 35:24–26)

6. Understanding the OT Theologies in the Psalms

The psalms of vengeance need to be understood in their historical context, which means reading them in the light of OT theologies. Some OT scholars use the concept of covenants (Abrahamic, Mosaic, and Davidic) to interpret the imprecatory psalms.[19] Besides the covenantal interpretation, I will show that pleas for vengeance could also be based on creation and Zion theologies.

John Day shows how Psalm 58 is built on the Mosaic covenant, while Psalm 109 recalls the Abrahamic covenant. He points out the similarity of language between Psalm 58 and the Song of Moses in Deuteronomy 32. Moses's Song functions as a witness of the covenant: it warns of God's punishment against Israel if they forsake him and also against their enemies if they oppress his people.[20] God's promise in Deuteronomy 32:35, "Vengeance is mine, I will repay," is taken up by Paul in Romans 12:19.

---

19. Johannes G. Vos, "The Ethical Problem of the Imprecatory Psalms," *Westminster Theological Journal* 4 (1942): 123–38; Chalmers Martin, "Imprecations in the Psalms," in *Classical Evangelical Essays in Old Testament Interpretation*, ed. Walter C. Kaiser (Grand Rapids: Baker, 1972), 113–32; Laney, "Fresh Look," 35–45; Allan M. Harman, "The Continuity of the Covenant Curses in the Imprecations of the Psalter," *The Reformed Theological Review* 54 (1995): 66–72; John Shepherd, "The Place of the Imprecatory Psalms in the Canon of Scripture: Part 2," *Churchman* 111, no. 2 (1997): 110–26. Daniel Simango and P. Paul Krüger, "An Overview of the Study of Imprecatory Psalms: Reformed and Evangelical Approaches to the Interpretation of Imprecatory Psalms," *Old Testament Essays* 29, no. 3 (2016): 592, write that "Baptist scholars like Spurgeon, Lockyer and Luc tend to favour the view that the imprecations are prophetic utterances, while Presbyterian and Reformed scholars, who emphasise the continuity between the Old and New Testaments, are inclined to view the imprecations as covenant curses. Among these Presbyterian and Reformed scholars are Vos, Martin, Harman, and Laney."

20. Day, *Crying for Justice*, 56–58.

Similarly, the Abrahamic covenant promised blessings to those who blessed God's people and curses to those who cursed them (Gen 12:1–3). Day notes that literary echoes of Genesis 12:3 are found in Psalm 109:28, where the enemy's "cursing" is contrasted with God's "blessing."[21] Paul appeals to the Abrahamic covenant in Galatians 3:6–29, making it applicable to Christians as well.

The Davidic covenant promises protection to the king by taking vengeance on his enemies.[22] This is seen in the Davidic psalm 143:12: "In your steadfast love cut off my enemies, and destroy all my adversaries, for I am your servant." As followers of Christ, the Son of David, his followers also enjoy the same protection.

Besides the above covenants,[23] I include creation and Zion theologies as other OT theological bases for the imprecatory psalms. The next chapter shows that Psalm 83 is built on creation theology. The Creator established an orderly cosmos and is appealed to as the universal King and Judge to defend the needy and establish justice over all the earth. This cry is found in Psalm 82:8: "Arise, O God, judge the earth; for you shall inherit all the nations!" (ESV). The fundamental principle of divine justice is encapsulated in the *lex talionis*, found three times in three different law codes: Exodus 21:23–25; Leviticus 24:19–20; and Deuteronomy 19:19–21:

> If any harm follows, then you shall give life for life, eye for eye, tooth for tooth, hand for hand, foot for foot, burn for burn, wound for wound, stripe for stripe. (Exod 21:23–25)

> Anyone who maims another shall suffer the same injury in return: fracture for fracture, eye for eye, tooth for tooth; the injury inflicted is the injury to be suffered. (Lev 24:19–20)

> . . . then you shall do to the false witness just as the false witness had meant to do to the other. So you shall purge the evil from

21. Day, 80.

22. Calvin, *Commentary on the Book of Psalms*, 258.

23. The three mentioned covenants are linked to their underlying OT theologies: the Abrahamic covenant is related to Priestly theology, Mosaic covenant to Deuteronomistic theology, and Davidic covenant to Zion theology. For further reading, see Bernhard W. Anderson, *Contours of Old Testament Theology* (Minneapolis: Fortress, 1999). While the Davidic covenant is based on Zion theology, the latter is independent of the former. Ben C. Ollenburger, *Zion, the City of the Great King: A Theological Symbol of the Jerusalem Cult*, JSOTSup 41 (Sheffield: JSOT, 1987), 49–66, argues that the Songs of Zion (Pss 46, 48, and 76) exalt God as king and make no mention of a human king.

your midst. The rest shall hear and be afraid, and a crime such as this shall never again be committed among you. Show no pity: life for life, eye for eye, tooth for tooth, hand for hand, foot for foot. (Deut 19:19–21)

Zion theology developed from creation theology but focused on the temple mount as God's throne. It is often related to the Davidic covenant, or it may focus only on God's kingship. The latter is the theme of the Songs of Zion (e.g. Pss 46, 47, 48). In chapter 10, I will show that the bashing of Babylonian infants in Psalm 137 is based on Zion theology.

While OT theologies help us understand the imprecatory psalms, these psalms also serve an emotional purpose as prayers.

7. Prayers of Dependence

"Dependence" is Nehrbass's term to describe the attitude of those who pray the curses: they do not take matters into their own hands but entirely depend on God to act.[24] He distinguishes dependence from catharsis, which is merely to ventilate one's pain and anger.[25] In fact, encouraging an angry person to keep dwelling on his or her negative thoughts would make that person more bitter.[26] The imprecatory psalms, however, direct us towards God and his justice.[27]

Erich Zenger points out that the imprecatory psalms are not prayed by people who have the power to effect a violent change in their situation of suffering. Instead, they surrender everything to God.[28] "They give *to God* not only their lament about their desperate situation, but also the right to judge the originators of that situation. They leave *everything* in God's hands, even feelings of hatred and aggression."[29]

---

24. Nehrbass, *Praying Curses*, 47.

25. Nehrbass, 25.

26. Dominick D. Hankle, "The Therapeutic Implications of the Imprecatory Psalms in the Christian Counseling Setting," *Journal of Psychology and Theology* 38, no. 4 (2010): 275.

27. Villanueva, *It's OK to Be Not OK*, 88–89, distinguishes between expressing anger and praying for punishment, implying that the former can be sufficiently therapeutic. However, both aspects are found in the imprecatory psalms and should be kept together. Anger is resolved when divine justice is certain.

28. Erich Zenger, *A God of Vengeance? Understand the Psalms of Divine Wrath* (Louisville: Westminster John Knox, 1996), 48.

29. Zenger, *God of Vengeance?*, 79 (emphasis original). He says that the strong language of the psalms teaches us that we can pray about "everything, literally everything, if only we say it to GOD."

Day adds that such prayers of bitter grief and anger may also "be offered for fellow brothers and sisters who are victims of widespread rape, murder, mutilation, and enslavement at the hands of a wicked regime. This is particularly so when none is willing or able to assist."[30] In other words, the psalms help us intercede with and for the suffering. They comfort the troubled and trouble the comfortable.

However, Nehrbass reminds us that dependence should not make us passive, but we are to do justice where we can.[31] The prophets indicted the powerful for neglecting the poor, Nehemiah rebuked the wealthy, and Esther risked her life for lives at risk. When we have committed the corrupt powers on earth to our Father in heaven, we can have the confidence to do his will on earth.

Conclusion

So, can a Christian pray the psalms of vengeance?

Although Lewis did not take the imprecatory psalms literally, still he said that these psalms remind us that the absence of indignation may be an alarming symptom of the decline of righteousness and moral conviction.[32]

At the beginning of the Second World War, Johannes G. Vos astutely wrote,

> God's kingdom cannot come without Satan's kingdom being destroyed. God's will cannot be done in earth without the destruction of evil. Evil cannot be destroyed without the destruction of men who are permanently identified with it. . . . Instead of being ashamed of the Imprecatory Psalms, and attempting to apologise for them and explain them away, Christian people should glory in them and not hesitate to use them in the public and private exercises of the worship of God.[33]

So yes, Christians *can* and *should* pray the psalms of vengeance. Of course, that means teaching the congregation about the biblical concepts of anger, forgiveness, and justice. It also means helping people appreciate the theologies contained in the imprecatory psalms, which we will unpack in the following three chapters.

---

30. Day, *Crying for Justice*, 72.
31. Nehrbass, *Praying Curses*, 48–49, 52.
32. Lewis, *Reflections on the Psalms*, 30.
33. Vos, "Ethical Problem," 138.

8

Psalm 83: Creation Theology[1]

Emma was fuming. Her boss, the senior pastor, had given a bad evaluation of her to the personnel committee. He reported she was not diligent when, in fact, she had done more than required – more Bible studies, more visitations, more teaching, more counselling – all without complaining.

The last straw came at a worship service. She arrived late to church because the public transport had broken down. At the end of the service, the pastor started berating people for coming late, and to her dismay, she heard her name mentioned. "I felt all eyes on me and heard some of them laughing," she recalled.

She told me that from that moment on, "I lost joy in going to Bible studies. There was so much anger and frustration in my heart. I wanted to take revenge for all the unfair things he accused me of. I could just let the congregation know what the lay leaders are complaining about him."

I suggested to Emma that she pour out her anger to God by journaling about her feelings. Two weeks later, she shared with me her journal, an extract of which I show below:

> Dear Lord, you are my defender and judge. Please defend me from the hands of my enemy. I cannot defend myself, but I trust you. I know you will vindicate me against those accusations and lies thrown against me. I am angry, Lord. I want him to be punished for treating me unfairly. I want him to feel what I am feeling now.

---

1. This chapter is adapted from my essay "Psalm 83: The Paradox of Cursing and Blessing," in *A Beautiful Life: Festschrift in Honour of Rev Dr Simon Chan on His 70th Birthday*, ed. Andrew Peh (Singapore: Graceworks, 2021), 89–99, and reproduced with permission from the publisher.

But I don't want to dwell in this kind of feeling for ever. I want you to deal with me. Give me love in my heart so that I can understand him. Give me love so that every time I think of revenge, I will think of doing good things for him instead. Help me to love my enemy and leave him to you.

Emma went on to tell me that three days after she wrote her journal, something unusual happened. She said,

I couldn't understand it. Instead of getting angry at him, I felt compassion for him. It was a strange feeling. When I was in church listening to him preach, I found myself praying for him. I prayed that we would all be ministered to by his sermon. I suddenly realized that he must be facing a lot of stress because he gets a lot of criticism from other church leaders, so I prayed for him that God would give him wisdom and strength.

In fact, after service that day, the pastor needed some help to pack up his office because the church was doing some renovations. So, without thinking, I just volunteered to help him. Together with another church member, we put his books into boxes and carried them into a storeroom. To my surprise, after we had finished, he invited the church member and me to his home for dinner. Since then, he has been talking nicely to me without being sarcastic.

Without realizing it, Emma had prayed like the psalmist in Psalm 83. After calling upon God and imprecating the enemy, she prayed that God would help her love her antagonist. God answered her prayer by changing her and the enemy.[2]

Psalm of Blessing and Cursing

Psalm 83 is a unique imprecatory psalm because it ends by cursing the enemies to death *and* blessing them to know God in the same breath:

> [16] Fill their faces with humiliation!
>   So that they may seek your name, O YHWH.
> [17] May they be put to shame and terrified for ever;
>   may they be disgraced and perish,

---

2. Admittedly, Emma could have spoken to her pastor about her conflicts with him, but she had shown love. His repentance may be implied by his change of behaviour, and her willingness to forgive resulted in a reconciled relationship.

[18] so that they may know that you, your name is YHWH, alone
the Most High over all the earth.[3]

The violent demands for destruction led a commentator to write, "This psalm is an unedifying and tedious catalogue of bloody violence. . . . These factors are largely responsible for the consensus that regards this psalm as one of the least religious of all the poems in the Psalter."[4] Nevertheless, I will show that if we understand it in the light of Old Testament creation theology, we can appreciate the legitimacy and beauty of this psalm.

What is creation theology? In the ancient Near East, there was a widespread belief in the *Chaoskampf* myth. The term means "battle against chaos," in which a god battles with the powers of chaos represented by the sea deity.[5] The god emerges victorious and is proclaimed king, thus establishing cosmic order, and in some versions, he goes on to create the world and humanity.[6] In the Hebrew Scriptures, YHWH is the creator and warrior, but unlike the Canaanite god Baal or the Mesopotamian equivalent Marduk, he simply commands the sea without having to do battle. By his establishing order over the cosmos and empowering the flourishing of life, natural order becomes the foundation for social and moral order. "Law, nature, and politics are only aspects of one comprehensive order of creation."[7]

Bernhard Anderson writes, "In this cosmic perspective, Israel's creation theology . . . was liberation theology." To quote George Landes, it was "a freeing of the ordered cosmos from the ever-present menace of primordial chaos, so that especially human social and political structures might be prevented from disintegration, the bonds of cohesion, cooperation, and stability maintained and strengthened, and continuity, social unity and solidarity ensured."[8]

---

3. The translations of Psalm 83 in this chapter are my own. YHWH is the Hebrew tetragrammaton for the name of God, translated as "LORD" in the English versions. It is pronounced as "Yahweh."

4. Edwin McNeill Poteat, "Exposition Psalms 42–89," in *Interpreter's Bible*, Vol. 4, *Psalms, Proverbs* (Nashville: Abingdon, 1955), 450–51.

5. The sea god is known as Yam in the Ugaritic Baal Cycle and Marduk in the Babylonian version, *Enuma Elish*.

6. Bernhard W. Anderson, "Introduction: Mythopoeic and Theological Dimensions of Biblical Creation Faith," in *Creation in the Old Testament*, ed. Bernhard W. Anderson (Philadelphia: Fortress, 1984), 2.

7. H. H. Schmid, "Creation, Righteousness, and Salvation: 'Creation Theology' as the Broad Horizon of Biblical Theology," in Anderson, *Creation in the Old Testament*, 105.

8. Anderson, "Introduction," 10; George Landes, "Creation and Liberation," in Anderson, *Creation in the Old Testament*, 136.

Thus, creation theology led to an understanding of God's universal, righteous reign. It also contains an eschatological hope that the entire world will do homage to YHWH as King.[9] Peoples who acknowledge him will flourish in peace, while those who rebel against his order will be punished by the unleashing of chaos. Hence, one can pray both for the enemies' extermination as well as for their enlightenment.

That Psalm 83 is based on creation theology is evident through two factors. First, it belongs to a collection known as the Psalms of Asaph (Pss 50, 73–83). Second, it uses vocabulary and images intrinsic to creation theology. These factors will be revealed through an exegesis of the psalm, covering its genre, poetry, and overall arrangement.

Genre Analysis

Imprecatory psalms may be understood as lament psalms with more extensive imprecations or curses.[10] The lament genre has a structure composed of the following basic elements:

- Complaints (about God, self, and enemy)
- Call to God for help
- Confession of sin or contention of innocence
- Curse of enemies
- Confidence in God
- Celebration (vow of thanksgiving)[11]

What biblical scholars mean by "complaints" is not grumbling but an honest pouring out to God about one's suffering. Thus, one can complain about God, enemies, and one's own pain. Note that not all the elements are always present in lament psalms.

Psalm 83 can be divided into two major parts, indicated by the pause (*selah*) at the end of verse 8. The first part complains to God about the enemies, and the second asks God to curse them. The two parts, analysed according to the structure of a lament psalm, are shown below.

---

9. Schmid, "Creation, Righteousness, and Salvation," 110.

10. Lucas, *Psalms and Wisdom Literature*, 61.

11. Tremper Longman III and Raymond B. Dillard, *An Introduction to the Old Testament*, 2nd ed. (Grand Rapids: Zondervan, 2007), 248.

First Part: Complaints (vv. 1–8)
Complaint about God
¹ O God, do not keep quiet; do not be silent,
    And do not be still, O God.
Complaint about enemies (with two reasons given)
² **Because** see, your enemies growl,
    and those who hate you have lifted their head.
³ **Against your people** they devise plans;
    and they conspire against your treasured ones. . . .
⁵ **Because** they consulted with a heart together;
    against you they make a covenant. . . .   v. 8 *Selah*

Second Part: Curses (vv. 9–18)
Curses against the enemies (with two comparisons)

⁹ Do to them **like** Midian, like Sisera,
    like Jabin at the Wadi Kishon! . . .
¹⁴ **Like** a fire that torches a thicket,
    and like a flame that flames mountains, . . .
Curses (with two emphases)
¹⁶ Fill their faces with humiliation!
    So that they may seek your name, O YHWH. . . .
¹⁸ **so that** they may know that you, your name is YHWH, alone
    the Most High over all the earth.

This is such an intense imprecatory psalm that the other elements are not explicit. There is no contention of innocence, except for the claim in verse 3 that the pray-ers are God's people. Neither is there the usual statement of confidence that God will deliver, though that is the assumption in the last line of the psalm that YHWH is the Most High over all the earth.

The complaints against the enemies list two reasons why God should act: they work against God's people and against God himself (vv. 3, 5). When asking God to punish the enemies, verses 9–15 appeal to what God has done in Israel's history and what God does in creation. In the final part of the imprecations, the reason for the enemies' humiliation is emphasized twice: "so that" they may seek and acknowledge YHWH.

Poetic Analysis

Verse 1

A Song. A Psalm of Asaph.
[1] O God, do not keep quiet;
> do not be silent,
> And do not be still, O God.

The psalm begins with a threefold appeal to God not to be silent. It is an implicit complaint about God not acting when he should.[12] Two reasons are given for this appeal, indicated by "because" in bold below:

Verses 2–8

[2] **Because** see, your enemies growl,
> and those who hate you have lifted their head.
[3] **Against your people** they devise plans;
> and they conspire against your treasured ones.
[4] They said, "Come, let us cut them off as a nation;
> and let not the name of Israel be remembered any more."
[5] **Because** they consulted with a heart together;
> **against you** they make a covenant –
[6] the tents of Edom and the Ishmaelites,
> Moab and the Hagrites,
[7] Gebal[13] and Ammon and Amalek,
> Philistia with the inhabitants of Tyre;
[8] Also Assyria joined them;
> they are the strong arm of the children of Lot.   *Selah*

The first reason in verse 2 is based on the enemies' attack on God's people, and as if that is not bad enough, the second reason makes this an attack against God himself. There is also a chiastic arrangement in this section.

A chiasm (from the Greek letter *chi* or "x") is a literary structure where ideas are repeated in reverse sequence, usually represented by letters – for example, A-B-B'-A'. The parallel thoughts are connected by similar Hebrew words, with the emphasis placed at the chiasm's centre.

---

12. Frank-Lothar Hossfeld and Erich Zenger, *Psalms*, Vol. 2, Hermeneia (Minneapolis: Fortress, 2005), 339.

13. John Goldingay, *Psalms*, Vol. 2, BCOTWP (Grand Rapids: Baker Academic, 2007), 578, discusses two possibilities for the identity of Gebal. It could be the northern city in Ezek 27:9, which would make a chiastic pairing with the city of Tyre. Another Gebal was a mountainous territory in Edom, which would link well with Ammon.

A ² your enemies
  B those who hate you
    C ³ against your treasured ones (Hebrew "hidden ones")
    C' ⁴ let us cut them off (Hebrew "cause to hide")
  B' ⁵ against you
A' ⁶⁻⁸ list of nine-plus-one enemies

The chiasm shows that while Israel are surrounded by their enemies in AA', they are still the centre of God's concern in CC'. There is a play of words in Hebrew between "treasured" (v. 3) and "cut off" (v. 4), based on the same root "hide": though the enemies seek to "hide" the people by destroying them, God "hides" and protects them as his treasure.[14]

Verses 6–8 list ten enemy nations. The first nine are smaller foes that surround Israel,[15] and Assyria brings the conflict to an international scale.[16] Zenger relates the nations to Egyptian iconography in which nine kings or nations represent the totality of hostile forces subjugated under the pharaoh's feet.[17] Thus, the reference to nine enemy nations portends their defeat by YHWH.

Verses 9–15 ask God to punish the enemies based on God's past victories (vv. 9–11) and his cosmic power (vv. 13–15). All the historical references are found in the Deborah and Gideon narratives (Judg 4–8), indicated in parentheses below:

---

14. Goldingay, *Psalms*, 2:576.

15. Edom, situated in the south-east of Judah, though most closely related to Israel as Jacob's brother, were an enemy from the time of the wilderness wanderings (Num 20) to the post-exilic period (Joel 4:19). The Ishmaelites, descendants of Ishmael, Isaac's rival stepbrother, were a nomadic group living in the south-east of Edom. Moab was the descendant of Lot, Abraham's nephew, but their enmity is shown by Balak trying to get the seer Balaam to curse Israel. The Hagrites form a parallel with the Ishmaelites, as Hagar was Ishmael's mother. Ammon, the brother of Moab, lies to the latter's north. Amalek in the south is another nomadic tribe, and in the south-west lies Philistia, both of which caused trouble for Israel from the time of the judges to the early monarchy. Gebal and Tyre make up the list of nine enemy nations (Goldingay, 2:578).

16. Goldingay, 2:579. Because Assyria (eighth–seventh century) is not known to support Israel's neighbours, Goldingay proposes that "Assyria" is used to denote Persia in the fifth century (cf. Ezra 6:22). In the period of Ezra and Nehemiah, Judah felt threatened by their neighbours who tried to sway the Persian king against them. "Children of Lot" is a pejorative term, since Lot's children, Moab and Ammon, were born out of incest. In the context, the term is also applied to Israel's other neighbours.

17. Hossfeld and Zenger, *Psalms*, 2:342.

Verses 9–15

[9] Do to them like Midian,	(**A** Gideon narrative)[18]
like Sisera, like Jabin at the Wadi	(**B** Deborah narrative)[19]
Kishon!	
[10] They perished at En-dor,	
they became dung for the ground.	
[11] Make their nobles like Oreb and like	(**A'** Gideon narrative)
Zeeb,	
and like Zebah and like Zalmunna	
all their princes!	
[12] Who said, "We will possess for our-	
selves the pastures of God."	
[13] O my God, make them like a whirl,	
like chaff before wind!	
[14] Like a fire that torches a thicket,	
and like a flame that flames mountains,	
[15] thus may you pursue them with your tempest,	
and with your whirlwind may you terrify them.	

The accounts in Judges were entrenched in Israel's tradition when God's power was most apparent to a beleaguered nation.[20] Israel experienced victory through unproven leaders like Deborah, the prophetess, and Gideon, the least of the weakest clan (Judg 4:4; 6:15).

Deborah's song in Judges 5 celebrates Israel's victory in terms of creation theology:

The stars fought from heaven,
from their courses they fought against Sisera.
The torrent Kishon swept them away,
the onrushing torrent, the torrent Kishon.
March on, my soul, with might! (Judg 5:20–21)

---

18. Midian in v. 9 is paralleled in v. 11 by the names Oreb, Zeeb, Zebah, and Zalmunna, leaders killed by Gideon in Judg 8.

19. Verses 9b–10 refer to Deborah and Barak's victory over King Jabin's general Sisera, who was routed at the Wadi Kishon in Judg 4–5. En-dor is between Wadi Kishon and Mt. Tabor, from where Barak advanced.

20. Hossfeld and Zenger, *Psalms*, 2:343. Isa 9:3 uses the Midianites' defeat for the eschatological hope of liberation from foreign oppression.

While human protagonists Barak and Jael did their part, it was God who destroyed the enemies through his control of nature. The rain and storm turned the Kishon valley into a raging torrent, overwhelming the enemy troops and their chariots. Victory comes from the Creator, who weaponizes the forces of chaos against his adversaries.

The events in verses 9–12 are not recounted chronologically: they begin with Gideon's triumph over the Midianites, turn back to Deborah's earlier victory over the Canaanites, and then return to the Midianites' defeat. This arrangement conveys the poetic effect of verse 13, with God swirling the enemies around like a whirl of chaff. Furthermore, the chiastic A-B-A' structure puts the enemies' death at the centre of the prayer in verses 9–12.

The supplication continues with similes of God's destruction: a fire that consumes not only a thicket but mountains, and a storm-wind that not only pursues but terrifies. Wind, fire, and storm are part of a theophany, that is, a manifestation of God's presence.[21] These natural phenomena display God's sovereignty over nature and nations. The focus on God as the creator explains the reference to the time of the judges when YHWH established the country through the nation's "primaeval" battles.[22]

In the last section, the enemies are cursed so that they may seek (*baqash*) YHWH.

Verses 16–18

A [16] Fill their faces with humiliation!
So that they may seek [*baqash*] **your name, O YHWH.**
B [17] May they be put to shame and terrified for ever;
may they be disgraced and perish,
A' [18] **so that** they may know that you, **your name** is **YHWH**, alone
the Most High over all the earth.

The Hebrew *baqash* implies seeking God in various contexts: in repentance (Deut 4:29), for help (2 Chr 20:4), or to follow his righteousness (Isa 51:1). Zechariah 8:22 is especially relevant, saying that "many peoples and strong nations shall come to seek [*baqash*] [YHWH] of hosts in Jerusalem, and to entreat the favour of [YHWH]." In other words, *baqash* in Psalm 83:16 implies that the psalmist is praying for his enemies' repentance by turning to God. Thus, Goldingay writes, "So it is for the truth's sake, for Yhwh's sake, that the

---

21. Hossfeld and Zenger, 2:344. Other theophanies involve fire at Mt. Sinai in Exod 19, fire and wind in Elijah's encounter at Sinai in 1 Kgs 19, and a whirlwind in Job 38 and 40.
22. Hossfeld and Zenger, 2:339.

psalm looks for this seeking, even if it will also be a blessing for the attackers themselves."[23]

The purpose ("so that")[24] of seeking YHWH's name is repeated in verses 16 and 18, forming an *inclusio* (A, A') surrounding the enemies in verse 17 (B). While the enemies had surrounded God's people in the chiasm of verses 2–8, the psalm ends with the enemies being surrounded by God. The central threat is that they will be destroyed unless they turn to YHWH, not only as the God of Israel but as the Most High over all the earth – that is, the universal creator-king.

Structural Analysis

The whole psalm can also be presented as a chiasm:

A [1] **O God**, do not keep quiet; do not be silent,   "God" 2x
And do not be still, **O God**.

    B [2] Because see, your enemies growl,
    and those who hate you have lifted their <u>head</u> . . .   head
    [4] They said, "Come, let us cut them off as a nation;
    and let not the *name* of Israel be remembered any   name
    more." . . .

        C [6] the tents of Edom and the Ishmaelites . . .   9 enemies
            D [8] Also Assyria joined them;
        C' [9] Do to them like Midian . . .   9 losers

    B' [16] Fill their *faces* with humiliation!   faces
    So that they may seek your *name*, **O YHWH** . . .   name

A' [18] so that they may know that you, your name is   "YHWH" 2x
YHWH . . .

The second half of the psalm reverses the first half. In AA', God was initially silent, but he will be known in the end. The generic "God" is revealed as YHWH, the sovereign God of Israel. In BB', those who lifted their "head" in pride will have their "faces" humiliated; those who sought to wipe out Israel's

---

23. Goldingay, *Psalms*, 2:582.

24. The Hebrew construction in vv. 16b and 18a where the imperative "fill" (v. 16a) and jussive "let them be put to shame" (v. 17) are followed by a conjunction *waw* with an imperfect verb ("seek" in v. 16b and "know" in v. 18a) should be translated as "so that." Also Goldingay, 3:584, n. 33.

"name" will have to seek YHWH's "name."[25] The pair CC' compares Israel's nine enemies with nine defeated foes and places. Assyria stands in the centre as a world power, but it is hemmed in by God, who controls all the earth.

Theological Analysis: Creation Theology

We can now discuss creation theology in Psalm 83, which is evident from the collection of Asaph psalms (50, 73–83) and from the content of Psalm 83 itself. First, the Asaph collection has a global perspective: God is the universal judge (Pss 50, 75, 76, and 82), and his justice is paralleled with the salvation of the oppressed in the world (Ps 76:10).[26] Like Psalm 83, other Asaph psalms appeal to all to call on YHWH's name and know him.[27] The title "Most High" ('elyon) is used eight times in the twelve Asaph psalms.[28] This divine epithet is used in contexts that show God's sovereignty over other gods and nations; for example, it was used by Melchizedek when Abraham defeated five foreign kings (Gen 14), by the foreign seer Balaam when he had to bless Israel (Num 24), and in Moses's song about God apportioning the nations (Deut 32).

This understanding of God's dominion stems from the Asaphite theology of God who creates (Ps 74 refers to the *Chaoskampf* myth) and upholds the earth (Ps 75). The psalms show God's power over nature through theophanies (Pss 50, 77, 83) and the exodus miracles (Ps 78). Christine Brown Jones argues that the Asaph psalms were written to address the confusion encountered after the destruction of the temple and the exile. "By highlighting God's role in the creation not only of Israel, God's chosen people, but of the entire cosmos, the Asaphite collection reminds the reader that God is sovereign over all and God remains powerful despite the defeat of the nation."[29]

Second, from Psalm 83 itself we find vocabulary and images related to creation theology. In the poetic analysis of the psalm, I pointed out that the reference to Deborah's victory was understood from a cosmic perspective: God's deliverance is described through the natural forces of wind, fire, and

---

25. Hossfeld and Zenger, *Psalms*, 2:339.

26. Christine Brown Jones, "The Message of the Asaphite Collection and Its Role in the Psalter," in *The Shape and Shaping of the Book of Psalms: The Current State of Scholarship*, ed. Nancy L. Declaisse-Walford (Atlanta: SBL, 2014), 73.

27. Hossfeld and Zenger, *Psalms*, 2:345. References to the knowledge of YHWH are found in Pss 73:11, 16, 22; 76:2; 77:15, 20; 78:3, 5, 6; 79:6; 82:5; references to the whole earth are found in Pss 50:1, 4; 73:25; 74:12, 17; 76:9, 10, 12; 78:69; 82:5, 8.

28. References to "Most High" ('elyon): Pss 50:14; 73:11; 77:10; 78:17, 35, 56; 82:6; 83:19.

29. Jones, "Asaphite Collection," 76.

storm, affirming his sovereignty over nature and nations. Such vocabulary and images are also found in other texts founded on creation theology.

The nations' "growl" (*hamah*) in Psalm 83:2 is used in Psalm 46, a Zion psalm, to describe the primaeval chaos of nature and nations:[30]

> Because see, your enemies growl [*hamah*],
> and those who hate you have lifted their head. (Ps 83:2)

> though its waters roar and foam,
> though the mountains tremble with its tumult
> [*hamah*] . . .
> The nations are in an uproar [*hamah*], the kingdoms totter;
> he utters his voice, the earth melts. (Ps 46:3, 6)

Like Psalm 83, Psalm 46 also concludes with God being acknowledged for his worldwide sovereignty.

Psalm 83 has even more in common with Isaiah 17:12–13 with its description of God's judgment on Assyria:[31]

> Ah, the thunder of many peoples,
> they thunder [*hamah*] like the thundering [*hamah*] of the
> sea! . . .
> The nations roar like the roaring of many waters,
> but he will rebuke them, and they will flee far away,
> <u>chased</u> like <u>chaff</u> on the <u>mountains</u> before the <u>wind</u>
> and <u>whirling dust</u> before the <u>storm</u>. (Isa 17:12–13)

The underlined words in Isaiah 17 above are also found in Psalm 83:

> O my God, make them like a <u>whirl</u>,
> like <u>chaff</u> before <u>wind</u>!
> Like a fire that torches a thicket,
> and like a flame that flames <u>mountains</u>,
> thus may you <u>pursue</u> them with your tempest,
> and with your <u>whirlwind</u> may you terrify them. (Ps 83:13–15)

The book of Isaiah is based on Zion theology, which is built on creation theology.[32] Regarding the conclusion of Psalm 83, Zenger writes, "The *attack of the nations* . . . becomes a *pilgrimage of the nations* (vv. 17b) and *homage of*

---

30. Hossfeld and Zenger, *Psalms*, 2:341. Also see Ps 65:7.

31. Hossfeld and Zenger, 2:341.

32. Maggie Low, *Mother Zion in Deutero-Isaiah: A Metaphor for Zion Theology*, Studies in Biblical Literature (New York: Peter Lang, 2013), 49–50.

the nations (v. 19)."[33] A similar global vision is laid out in Isaiah 2:2–4, where God will judge between nations and establish peace. Because creation theology calls attention to YHWH's universal just and life-giving reign, the psalmist can thus pray both for the destruction of God's enemies and also for their salvation.[34] Psalm 83 is "fundamentally missional in nature."[35]

Conclusion

This unique psalm shows us how to apply Romans 12:14–21 with its call to bless our enemies while leaving vengeance to God. Villanueva points out that when Christians pray only blessing, including for corrupt powers, it shows that we are ignorant or apathetic about justice. Writing in the Philippines context, he cites an election official who told him that "the reason why the government is not afraid of Christians is because we only pray for blessings; we are so nice. We do not know how to get angry."[36]

While Psalm 83 is about external enemies, what about those within the household of faith? The OT shows that God punishes his own people when they oppress others. In the NT, 1 Peter 4:17 warns that judgment begins with the household of God. God's impartiality explains why Emma could also pray this psalm when her senior pastor mistreated her.

The most vital motivation to pray Psalm 83 is that all may acknowledge YHWH, whether as salvation for unbelievers or sanctification for Christ's disciples. For those who backstab, cheat, or abuse us, for those who commit rape, terrorism, or genocide, we cast them upon the judgment of the Most High that they might be convicted to seek the Creator of all. Zenger concludes, "It is significant that these petitions are shouted to God, leaving it to him how he will act."[37]

---

33. Zenger, *God of Vengeance?*, 45 (emphasis original).

34. These two requests seem incongruous, for if the enemies die, how can they seek YHWH? It may be that the destruction of an army becomes a testimony to its remaining survivors and civilians.

35. W. Dennis Tucker, Jr., and Jamie A. Grant, *Psalms*, Vol. 2, NIVAC (Grand Rapids: Zondervan, 2018), 239.

36. Villanueva, *It's OK to Be Not OK*, 90–91.

37. Hossfeld and Zenger, *Psalms*, 2:340.

9

Psalm 109:
Covenant Theologies[1]

In a corner of a McDonald's restaurant, Chrissie shared a painful secret: she had been sexually abused by her older brother when she was young. She had told her mum, who not only refused to believe her but even accused her of lying about her brother. The abuse continued until he decided to stop because she would always break down crying.

Chrissie grew up trying to prove herself to her mum, and eventually she fell into depression. That day, I brought her out for a chat, and it was then that she shared what she had never told anyone before.

"Have you ever told God about what your brother did?" I asked.

"No," she replied. "I want to forget about it."

"But obviously, it's affecting you still," I pointed out. "Let's bring it to God."

Chrissie agreed. I prompted her to tell God how she felt about what her brother did. Like most Christians, she started with, "Lord, I forgive my brother." I redirected her to begin with her feelings. She went quiet; her eyes shut tight, her hands clenched. Then the tears started streaming down her face, and she couldn't stop.

I waited for the years of pain and repressed rage to be released. It wasn't just her brother she was angry with, she was even more hurt by her mum – the one person she thought would protect her but who had turned against her. Psalm 109 is for someone like Chrissie, who has been abused, betrayed, and falsely accused.

---

1. I use the plural "theologies" to refer to the different types of covenants in the Old Testament, with their different theological emphases. For Ps 109, two covenants are relevant: the Abrahamic covenant and the Mosaic covenant. For more discussion, see Anderson, *Contours of Old Testament Theology*.

However, in church history, Psalm 109 has been misused to "pray people to death." John Calvin excoriated monks who could be paid to recite this psalm daily against one's enemies.[2] During the eighteenth century, some people believed that if this psalm were prayed without interruption for one year and nine days, it would have a deadly effect on the victim.[3] In their commentary, Dennis Tucker and Jamie Grant write that contemporary American Christians have been invited to use this psalm against political leaders with whom they disagreed, especially the line "May his days be few; may another take his place of leadership" (Ps 109:8).[4] Against such misuse, we need to understand the psalm's appeal for *lex talionis* based on the Abrahamic and Mosaic covenants.

Genre and Structural Analysis

The following is a genre analysis of Psalm 109 as a lament psalm. Structurally, there are three parts: a call to God complaining about false accusations, an extended segment of cursing, and a final section expressing confidence in God, which includes calls for help, curses, and celebration.[5]

Part 1: Call to God (vv. 1–5)
Call to God for help
[1] O God of my praise, do not be silent,
Complaint against the enemies
[2] For a wicked mouth and a deceitful mouth opened against
   me . . .
Contention of innocence
[4] In place of my love they accuse me . . .

Part 2: Curses against the enemy (vv. 6–19)
Curses against the enemy and his family
[8] May his days be few;
his appointment be taken by another.
[9] May his children be orphans,
and his wife a widow . . .

2. John Calvin, *Psalms*, Vol. 4, Calvin's Commentaries, trans. James Anderson (Grand Rapids: Eerdmans, 1949), 276. Calvin believed that the curses were spoken by David acting as a type of Christ. The words are also for members of Christ's church to ask God for vengeance when unjustly treated by enemies (268).

3. Zenger, *God of Vengeance?*, 57–58.

4. Tucker and Grant, *Psalms*, 2:587.

5. The translations of Psalm 109 in this chapter are my own.

Reasons for the curses against the enemy
[16] Because he did not remember to do steadfast love,
but pursued the poor and needy and the broken-hearted to
    death . . .

Part 3: Confidence in God (vv. 20–31)
Confidence in God's help
[20] This the payment of my accusers, from YHWH,
of those who speak evil against my life.
Call for help
[21] And you, O YHWH my Lord, you act with me on account of
    your name! . . .
Confidence in God's help
[27] You, YHWH, you have done it.
Curse of enemies
[28] . . . May they arise and be ashamed . . .
Celebration
[30] I will give thanks to YHWH greatly with my mouth . . .

The Crux: Who Is the Speaker of Psalm 109:6–19?

The crux of the psalm is whether the deadly curses are spoken by the psalmist or his enemies. If spoken by the psalmist, then Christians may also utter such vicious words. To avoid the harshness, some interpreters take the curses as the psalmist's quotations of the enemies' verbal attacks against himself. I list eight arguments below for both views, leading to my conclusion that the imprecations have a double meaning: the psalmist uses his enemies' words against them in the end.

1. Singular References to an Enemy in 109:6–19

There is a change between the plural pronouns used for the psalmist's enemies in verses 2–5 and 20–31, and the singular references used in verses 6–19. Some scholars argue that the singular can refer to the enemies as a group or specifically to the ringleader. Also, certain psalms use the plural and the collective singular for enemies in the same text (Pss 35:8, 10; 27:12).[6] However,

---

6. Leslie C. Allen, *Psalms 101–150*, rev. ed., WBC (Nashville: Thomas Nelson, 2002), 102–3, discusses these arguments but finds that the consistent singular references in vv. 6–19 are suggestive of it being a quotation. David P. Wright, "Ritual Analogy in Psalm 109," *Journal*

others find that the use of the singular in Psalm 109:6–19 is "particularly clean," meaning that these are words directed against the lone psalmist.[7]

2. Indirect Reference to God in 109:6–19

God is addressed directly in the first and third parts, but only indirectly in verses 6–19. In individual laments, the psalmist's wishes for retribution are always expressed directly to God (e.g. Ps 69:22–28), but quotations of enemies' words only refer to God indirectly in the third person (e.g. Pss 3:2; 22:8; 71:11).[8]

3. References to the Accusers' Words in 109:1–4

Many psalms quote the enemies' words without introducing them (e.g. Pss 2:3; 22:8; 10:4) and these must be determined by the context. In 109:4–5, the psalmist argues for his innocence, and therefore verses 6–19 may be his own words. Yet, verses 2–3 refer to the enemies' speech: "mouth" (repeated twice), "they spoke," "tongue," "words of hate," and "accuse." Thus, verses 6–19 may also reprise the accusers' words.

4. Request for a Wicked Accuser in Verse 6

The request for a wicked person to be the prosecutor, thus ensuring a conviction even by unjust means, may be a request for *lex talionis*, since the adversaries falsely accused the victim in the first place (vv. 2, 4). However, such a corrupt appeal is more suited as coming from the mouth of the wicked.

---

of Biblical Literature 113, no. 3 (1994): 394, lists examples of psalms that refer to enemies in both the singular and the plural, but they are scattered in the respective psalms.

7. John Goldingay, *Psalms*, Vol. 3, *Psalms 90–150*, BCOTWP (Grand Rapids: Baker Academic, 2008), 279.

8. Allen, *Psalms 101–150*, 104, citing P. Hugger, "'Das sei meiner Ankläger Lohn . . .'? Zur Deutung von Ps. 109:20," *Bibel und Leben* 14 (1973): 111 (105–12). Admittedly, v. 20 ("This the payment of my accusers, from YHWH"), which is usually regarded as spoken by the psalmist, refers to YHWH in the third person, but it is followed immediately by a prayer directly to YHWH in the next verse.

5. Repeated Words in 109:2–5//109:20

The words set below in bold show where the same words are used in the two segments surrounding verses 6–19:

> [1] O God of my praise, do not be silent,
>> [2] For a wicked mouth and a deceitful mouth opened against me.
> They **spoke** with me a lying tongue,
>> [3] And words of hate surrounded me,
>> and attacked me for no reason.
> [4] In place of my love they **accuse** me,
>> but I a prayer.
>> [5] And they set against me **evil** in place of good
> and hatred in place of my love.
> . . .
>> [20] This the payment of my **accusers**, from YHWH,
>> of those who **speak** evil against my life.

Verse 20 shows that the psalmist's imprecations are just payment for his antagonists' abuse. However, the repeated words before and after verses 6–19 function like open and closed quotation marks, indicating that the psalmist was referring to his accusers' remarks.[9]

6. Referent of "Curse" in Verse 28

In verse 28, the psalmist says, "May they curse, they, but you, you will bless." This "curse" refers back to verse 17: "He loved to curse; let curses come on him." Thus, it seems that the psalmist is referring to the enemies' cursing in verses 6–19. However, verses 6–19 may also be taken as the verbatim report of the enemies' "curse" mentioned in verse 28.[10]

---

9. Stephen Egwim, "Determining the Place of vv. 6–19 in Ps 109: A Case Presentation Analysis," *Ephemerides Theologicae Lovanienses* 80, no. 1 (2004): 114.

10. Egwim, "Vv. 6–19 in Ps 109," 115.

7. References to the "Poor and Needy" (vv. 16, 22)

Verse 16, "he pursued the poor and needy," seems an appropriate reference to the psalmist as the victim, who describes himself as such in verse 22.[11] However, to pursue the poor is a serious offence before God and could be a false charge by the psalmist's enemies. Verse 22 is then the psalmist's defence that, rather than pursuing the poor, he is "the poor" who is being attacked.

8. Citation in the NT

Peter in Acts 1:20 applies Psalm 109:8 to Judas: "Let another take his position." This judgment seems to imply that Peter regarded verses 6–19 as the psalmist's requests.[12] Even so, the context of the psalm demonstrates the principle of *lex talionis*, for just as Judas demanded Jesus's removal, so he himself was removed from his position.

In sum, scholars are evenly divided in this debate, but this only goes to show the likely double meaning of the psalm. Verse 20, "this the payment of my accusers, from YHWH," is the pivotal key – that is, verses 6–19 begin as a quotation of the enemies' allegations, but in the light of verse 20, the psalmist turns his opponents' words against them on the basis of *lex talionis*.[13] Whatever judgment they sought against the innocent victim will be executed against them. For the reader, the curses are not directly one's own requests but examples of vengeance, so victims can ask God to return their enemies' harm back upon them.

We now continue with the poetic analysis of Psalm 109.

Poetic Analysis

The principle of *lex talionis* is demonstrated by many artful reversals in the psalm. God will establish justice for the psalmist even when judges, prosecutors,

---

11. Egwim, 126–27, explains that in the Psalms, "poor" (*'oni*) is a spiritual term more than an economic one. It does not necessarily describe the materially poor but those who are oppressed, helpless, and, thus, dependent on God.

12. Day, *Crying for Justice*, 77.

13. Villanueva, *It's OK to Be Not OK*, 87–88, takes vv. 6–19 as the psalmist's words. He says that by his honest utterance, the psalmist is able to praise God in the end. Rather, genre analysis shows that the change comes in v. 20 when the psalmist declares his confidence in God's justice. The imprecatory psalms provide not just psychological relief but theological assurance. However, Villanueva, 91–93, does emphasize punishment against the wicked from Pss 52 and 10 in particular.

and witnesses are corrupt. When there is no justice in human courts, we can confidently appeal to the heavenly court.

> *Part 1: Call to God (vv. 1–5)*
> To the leader. Of David. A Psalm.
> ¹ O God of my praise, do not be silent,
>> ² For a wicked mouth and a deceitful mouth opened
>> against me.
> They spoke with me a lying tongue,
>> ³ And words of hate surrounded me,
>> and attacked me for no reason.
> ⁴ *In place of my love* they accuse me,
>> but I a prayer.
>> ⁵ And they set against me evil in place of good
> and hatred *in place of my love.*

The psalmist begins by pleading with God not to be silent because of his enemies' verbal attacks. Verses 4–5 are a four-line chiastic arrangement with the repetition of "in place of my love" (italicized above). Though words of hate surrounded him (v. 3a), he encircled his enemies with love and goodness. "But I a prayer" in verse 4b is enigmatic: it could mean that the psalmist prays *for* his accusers (just as in Ps 35:13) or *against* them.[14] Though both are possible, the psalmist's love suggests that he is interceding for their benefit.[15] As in Psalm 83, the psalmist acts with enemy love, and he also entrusts justice to God.

> *Part 2: Curses against the enemy (vv. 6–19)*
> *Curses against the enemy and his family (vv. 6–15)*
> ⁶ Appoint against him a wicked one,
>> and an accuser let him stand on his right.
> ⁷ When he is judged, let him go forth wicked,
>> let his prayer be as sin.
> ⁸ May his days be few;
>> his appointment be taken by another.
> ⁹ May his children be *orphans,*
>> and his wife a widow;

---

14. Goldingay, *Psalms*, 3:279, takes it as the suppliant appealing to the court.

15. A. A. Anderson, *Psalms*, Vol. 2, *73–150*, NCB (Grand Rapids: Eerdmans, 1972), 760, writes that "love" (*'ahav*) means "deep friendship."

¹⁰ and wandering may his children wander and beg,
  and driven from their ruins.
  ¹¹ May the creditor strike at all that he has;
  and strangers plunder his property.
  ¹² May there be no one drawing for him steadfast love,
  nor anyone being gracious to his *orphans*.
  ¹³ May his posterity be *cut off*;
  in another generation, may it be blotted out their name.
  ¹⁴ May it be remembered the iniquity of his father to
  YHWH,
  and the sin of his mother not be blotted out.
  ¹⁵ May they be before YHWH continually,
  and may it be *cut off* from the earth their memory.

In this second part, verse 6 turns to the court for judgment.[16] Verses 6–7 pick up several words from verses 1–5 (shown in bold below):

¹ O God of my praise, do not be silent,
  ² For a **wicked** mouth and a deceitful mouth opened
  against me.
They spoke with me a lying tongue,
  ³ And words of hate surrounded me,
  and attacked me for no reason.
⁴ In place of my love they **accuse** me,
  but I a **prayer**.
  ⁵ And they set **against me** evil in place of good
and hatred in place of my love.
. . .
⁶ Appoint against him a wicked one,
  and an **accuser** let him stand on his right.
⁷ When he is judged, let him go forth **wicked**,
  let his **prayer** be as sin.

In verse 6, it seems that the psalmist is asking for retribution against his enemies. However, the startling request for a dishonest prosecutor and

---

16. Goldingay, *Psalms*, 3:280, 282, believes that it is the heavenly court rather than an earthly one because the punishment of cutting off (vv. 13, 15) suggests God's action rather than human action.

the shift from plural to a singular enemy indicate that these are likely the accusers' words.

Verses 9–12 are set in a chiastic arrangement with "orphans" as an *inclusio* (italicized above). Not only are his children orphaned, but they will be left with nothing to live on and no one to help them. His children and wife would be the collateral damage of the man's demise.[17] Another chiasm is formed by verses 13–15, with "cut off" repeated (italicized above). The desire is to see the accused's lineage wiped out in this life and for ever, beginning with the punishment of his sinful parents.[18] The accused's sins are then set out in verses 16–19.

> *Reasons for the curses against the enemy (vv. 16–19)*
> [16] Because he did not remember to do steadfast love,
>> but pursued the poor and needy and the broken-hearted
>> to death,
> [17] and he loved a curse, so it entered him;
>> and he did not delight in blessing, and it was far from
>> him.
> [18] and he clothed himself with a curse as his coat,
>> so it entered like water into him, and like oil into his
>> bones.
> [19] May it be for him like the robe that he wraps around,
>> like the belt that he girds on.

Verses 16–19 give the reasons for the imprecations. There will be no memory of the accused's family (v. 15) because he supposedly did not remember to show steadfast love but cursed others.

Part 3: Confidence in God (vv. 20–31)
Confidence in God
> **A** [20] This the payment of my accusers, from YHWH,
>> of those who speak evil against my life.
> *Call for help*
> **B** [21] And you, YHWH my Lord, act with me on account of
>> your name!

---

17. So also Goldingay, 3:281.

18. See ch. 4 regarding the punishment to the third and fourth generations. The punishment in Exod 34:7 and Deut 5:9 refers either to the consequences of sin or to the continuation of the sinful act by the succeeding generations. In Ps 109, it is the latter, since both the accused and his parents are regarded as having sinned.

For good is <u>your steadfast love</u>, deliver me!
> *Complaint about self (vv. 22–25)*
> **C** ²² For poor and needy am ***I***,
>> and my heart is pierced within me.
> ²³ Like a shadow when it lengthens, I am gone;
>> I am shaken off like a locust.
> ²⁴ My knees stumble from hunger;
>> my flesh wastes away without fat.
> **C'** ²⁵ And ***I***, I am an object of scorn to them;
>> when they see me, they shake their head.
> *Call for help*
> **B'** ²⁶ Help me, <u>YHWH my God</u>!
> Save me according to <u>your steadfast love</u>!
> *Confidence in God*
> **A'** ²⁷ And let them know that <u>this</u> is your hand;
>> You, YHWH, you have done it.

Part 3 is arranged chiastically with the psalmist's complaint about his suffering in the centre (C, C'). The independent pronoun "I" (bold italics above) is repeated in verses 22 and 25. The psalmist says that he is the poor and needy person, not the one pursuing the poor and needy (v. 16). He is the one suffering inwardly with a pierced heart, outwardly from hunger and wasting, and socially as an object of scorn. However, in BB', he calls on YHWH's steadfast love for help, and in AA', he is surrounded by confidence in YHWH's answer.[19] The structural arrangement of this section shows that God's help and love now encompass the psalmist, in contrast to the enemies' words surrounding him in verse 3.

Verse 20 is the turning point, indicated by the plural "accusers" in contrast to the singular evildoer in verses 6–19. It also returns to the first person singular "I, me, my" used in verses 1–5. Furthermore, there is the direct appeal to God in the second person ("God of my praise," "my Lord," "my God"). In contrast, verses 6–19 referred to God in the third person (vv. 14 and 15) as part of "conventional uses."[20]

---

19. The repeated words in the chiastic pairs are indicated by underlining. In AA', "this" (feminine singular pronoun in vv. 20 and 27) refers to God's repayment (*pe'ullah*, a feminine singular noun); in BB', "YHWH my Lord/God," "your steadfast love," and two pairs of imperatives (indicated by exclamation marks) are used.

20. Goldingay, *Psalms*, 3:279.

Verse 20 is a verbless clause and may be interpreted in the future or present. The future translation, "May this be the payment of my accusers from YHWH," is found in most English versions. Goldingay also explains this as a wish by the pray-er that the evil words will be turned back upon his enemies.[21] However, in the context of a lament psalm, verse 20 can also be considered as a statement of confidence and, thus, be translated in the present tense: "This *is* the payment of my accusers from YHWH." This reading is reflected in the parallel verse 27, which uses the Hebrew perfect "you have done it," expressing a completed action. God's retribution is as good as done, whether it happens now or in the future.

> *Curse of the enemies (vv. 28–29)*
> [28] May they curse [*qalal*], they,
>   but you, you will bless.
> May they arise and be ashamed,
>   but your servant, may he rejoice.
> [29] May my accusers be clothed with dishonour;
>   and may they be wrapped as in a robe in their shame.

Part 3 of the psalm continues with imprecations, asking that the malicious accusers be put to shame. Verse 28 contrasts what his enemies do with what God can do. It recalls the Abrahamic promise in Genesis 12:3: when God's people were "cursed" (*qalal*), God promised to "curse" the enemies.

Verses 26–29 neatly reverse what the accusers said about the psalmist in verses 16–19. The repeated words in the two sections are shown below in bold:

> [16] Because he did not remember to do **steadfast love**,
>   but pursued the poor and needy and the broken-hearted
>   to death,
> [17] and he loved a **curse**, so it entered him;
>   and he did not delight in **blessing**, and it was far from
>   him.
> [18] and he **clothed** himself with a curse as his coat,
>   so it entered like water into him, and like oil into his
>   bones.
> [19] May it be for him like the robe that he **wraps** around,
>   like the belt that he girds on.

---

21. Goldingay, 3:285.

. . .

²⁶ Help me, YHWH, my God!
 Save me according to your **steadfast love**!
²⁷ And let them know that this is your hand;
 you, YHWH, you have done it.
²⁸ May they **curse**, they,
 but you, you will **bless**.
May they arise and be ashamed,
 but your servant, may he rejoice.
²⁹ May my accusers be **clothed** with dishonour;
 and may they be **wrapped** as in a mantle in their shame.

Being protected by God's steadfast love, the psalmist now prays that God will reverse all the enemies' attacks. They said he did not show steadfast love, but he appeals to God's steadfast love. They accused him of cursing, but he points out that they are the ones cursing. They said he did not bless others, but he trusts that God will bless him. They said he clothed himself with cursing and would be wrapped in it, a fate that he wishes back on them.

Celebration (vv. 30–31)
³⁰ I will give thanks to YHWH greatly with my **mouth**,
 And in the midst of many I will **praise** him.
³¹ For he **stands on the right** of the needy,
 to save from the **judges** of his life.

The psalm ends with celebration and thanksgiving. These last two verses recall verses 1–7, with the repeated words in bold shown below:

¹ O God of my **praise**, do not be silent,
 ² For a wicked **mouth** and a deceitful **mouth** opened
  against me.

 . . .

⁶ Appoint against him a wicked one,
 and an accuser let him **stand on his right**.
⁷ When he is **judged**, let him go forth wicked,
 let his prayer be as sin.

Instead of complaining about God's silence and the mouth of the wicked, the psalmist now gives thanks and praise to YHWH with his own mouth. His change of attitude is possible because, in place of his accuser on the right,

YHWH now stands on his right to defend him, and instead of being judged, he is saved from the judges.

Theological Analysis: Covenant Theologies

Psalm 109 appeals to both the Abrahamic and Mosaic covenants.[22]

1. The Abrahamic Covenant

Regarding the Abrahamic covenant, blessings and curses are promised in Genesis 12:3:

> Now the LORD said to Abram, "Go from your country and your kindred and your father's house to the land that I will show you. I will make of you a great nation, and I will bless you, and make your name great, so that you will be a blessing. I will bless those who bless you, and the one who curses [*qalal*] you I will curse [*'arar*];[23] and in you all the families of the earth shall be blessed." (Gen 12:1–3)

God will bless those who bless Abraham, while those who curse (*qalal*, meaning "disdain") him will be cursed (*'arar*, meaning divine destruction). In Psalm 109, "curse" (*qalal*) is used three times and "bless" twice. Verses 17–18 wish for the curser to be cursed. Although the enemy did not like to bless (v. 17) but curse (v. 28), God himself will bless the psalmist (v. 28), as promised in Genesis 12:2.

The Abrahamic covenant also applies in the NT to people of faith, as Paul showed in Galatians 3:6–29:

> Just as Abraham "believed God, and it was reckoned to him as righteousness," so, you see, those who believe are the descendants of Abraham. And the scripture, foreseeing that God would justify

---

22. Day, *Crying for Justice*, 79–81, appeals to these two covenants on the basis of Gen 12:1–3 and Exod 34:7. I add Deut 19:16–21 as further evidence for the Mosaic covenant.

23. Gen 12:3b, "and the one who curses [*qalal*] you I will curse [*'arar*]," has a disrupted syntax in Hebrew with the noun rather than the verb occurring at the beginning of the clause. Further, it focuses on a singular "one cursing you" in contrast to the plural "those blessing you." Thus, I agree with Patrick D. Miller, "Syntax and Theology in Genesis XII 3a," *Vetus Testamentum* 34 (1984): 472–76, who argues that Gen 12:3b is better understood as a parenthetical promise of protection for God's people. Mathews, *Genesis*, 116, disagrees, arguing that Gen 12:3a, b forms a chiasmus, but this interpretation would not fit God's ultimate purpose to bless the world.

the Gentiles by faith, declared the gospel beforehand to Abraham, saying, "All the Gentiles shall be blessed in you." For this reason, those who believe are blessed with Abraham who believed . . . in order that in Christ Jesus the blessing of Abraham might come to the Gentiles, so that we might receive the promise of the Spirit through faith. . . . And if you belong to Christ, then you are Abraham's offspring, heirs according to the promise. (Gal 3:6–9, 14, 29)

Thus, Christians are Abraham's heirs and receive God's blessing of righteousness through Christ. So, also, we inherit the promise of protection: "It is . . . just of God to repay with affliction those who afflict you" (2 Thess 1:6).

2. The Mosaic Covenant

The appeal to the Mosaic covenant can be seen in three ways: the promise of punishment upon children, the law against malicious accusers, and the principle of *lex talionis*.

First, the imprecations against children and parents in Psalm 109:9–15 rely on God's revelation to Moses in Exodus 20:5–6 (//Deut 5:9) and 34:7: "visiting the iniquity of the parents upon the children and the children's children, to the third and the fourth generation." As discussed in chapter 4, this declaration is not about the punishment of innocent descendants but the consequences of sin, especially if family members follow in their elders' footsteps. Thus, the accused's wife and children are not said to be guilty but suffer as a consequence of his wrongs, while his sinful parents are to be punished like him.

Second, there is also an appeal to the Mosaic law, given the judicial setting of the psalm. The court scene is described with God as the judge, and legal terms are used – for example, "appoint" an "accuser" "on his right" (the prosecutor) and "to go forth as wicked" (the guilty conviction).[24] Psalm 109:20 applies the law against a malicious witness:[25]

If a malicious witness comes forward to accuse someone of wrongdoing, then both parties to the dispute shall appear before the LORD, before the priests and the judges who are in office in those days, and the judges shall make a thorough inquiry. If the witness is a false [*sheqer*] witness, having testified falsely against

---

24. Egwim, "Vv. 6–19 in Ps 109," 117.
25. Egwim, 125.

another, then you shall do to the false witness just as the false witness had meant to do to the other. So you shall purge the evil from your midst. The rest shall hear and be afraid, and a crime such as this shall never again be committed among you. Show no pity: life for life, eye for eye, tooth for tooth, hand for hand, foot for foot. (Deut 19:16–21)

The psalmist described his enemies speaking with a lying (*sheqer*) tongue in Psalm 109:2, thus acting as the false (*sheqer*) witness of Deuteronomy 19:18. Therefore, the accusers who sought his death (Ps 109:8, 16, 20) deserved death.

Third, the law against false witnesses is based on *lex talionis* (Deut 19:21).[26] The poetic analysis of the psalm illustrates this principle through several patterns of reversal, with Psalm 109:20 as the pivot proclaiming YHWH's repayment:

- The psalmist, who was surrounded by words of hate (v. 3), is ultimately surrounded by God's vindication in (vv. 20, 27).
- The one who prayed for his enemies with love (vv. 4–5) but was accused of not practising steadfast love (v. 16) will be answered by God's steadfast love (vv. 21, 26).
- The enemies' curses on the victim (vv. 16–19) will return upon them (vv. 26–29).
- In place of a corrupt persecutor, YHWH is the psalmist's protector on his right (vv. 6, 31), and instead of being judged guilty, YHWH saves him from judges who condemn him (vv. 7, 31).

In the NT, Paul also relied on the principle of *lex talionis*: for example, in 2 Timothy 4:14, "Alexander the coppersmith did me great harm; the Lord will pay him back for his deeds." The new covenant continues the principle of just retribution from the Mosaic covenant, with Romans 12:19 and Hebrews 10:30 affirming the vengeance promised in the Song of Moses (Deut 32:35, 41, 43).

---

26. *Lex talionis* is found throughout the Torah (Exod 21:24; Lev 24:20) and it is also the basis for other ancient Near Eastern laws, such as the early second-millennium Code of Hammurabi. The belief in justice and fairness is rooted in the character of God, particularly as one who created the world and established its physical, social, and moral order. See Schmid, "Creation, Righteousness, and Salvation," 104.

Conclusion

Erich Zenger describes Psalm 109 not as a "cursing psalm" but as a "justice psalm."[27] Brueggemann argues that such angry prayers should not be censored lest the rage be repressed and left to fester or be expressed in violence. Rather, it should be relinquished to God, which means trusting God to act in God's way and timing. Then the victim is set free to live unencumbered. "Psalm 109, then, is a marvellous act of liberation."[28]

This is a liberation that Chrissie eventually found. After crying her heart out in that McDonald's restaurant, her words of agony stumbled out in prayer. We brought her abuse and betrayal to Jesus, the one who also suffered physical torment and false accusations that led to death. She entrusted her vindication to the sovereign judge: he will shame the brother who shamed her, and he will convict the mother who accused her. She left her brother and mother in God's hands.[29] When we had finished praying, she felt an overwhelming sense of peace because she had made the psalmist's words her own: "Help me, YHWH, my God! Save me according to your steadfast love! And let them know that this is your hand; you, YHWH, you have done it."

---

27. Hossfeld and Zenger, *Psalms*, 3:138. Goldingay, *Psalms*, 3:289, sees God's wrath as the foundation for moral and social order.

28. Walter Brueggemann, *The Message of the Psalms: A Theological Commentary* (Minneapolis: Augsburg, 1984), 85–86. His view is that vv. 6–19 are the psalmist's words, but his conclusion is still valid.

29. This is the beginning of healing and reconciliation for those like Chrissie. She needed to take the step of speaking to her brother and mother about the abuse, but regardless of whether they repented, she could be assured that God would take care of the matter in his justice.

10

Psalm 137:
Zion Theology

3 June 1989. A quiet Saturday in Hong Kong. Twenty-nine-year-old Pastor Ho was listening closely to the radio. Students had been gathering in Tiananmen Square in Beijing in a pro-democracy movement, calling for greater accountability and freedom of speech. At the height of the protests, about one million people assembled in the Square.[1]

The Chinese government had tried conciliatory tactics with the students but eventually called for a military solution to end the standoff. Troops and tanks rolled into the city. On that fateful Saturday night, shots rang out, at first into the air, but when the people resisted, the shots were aimed directly at the crowds. Pastor Ho heard those shots blasted over the radio, piercing his ears and heart. On Sunday, 4 June, the live telecast abruptly ended in the early morning.

The newly minted pastor spent the night frenziedly tuning the radio for updates. He was supposed to prepare for his sermon that Sunday, but he could not focus. He decided to go early to the church; at least he could spend time in prayer. As he trudged his way there, he worried about church members who had family and friends in China. When he arrived at the sanctuary, he found his senior pastor kneeling at the altar.

"What shall we do?" Pastor Ho blurted. "Everyone is worried sick about the situation in China. I don't think what I have prepared for my sermon is appropriate. I don't know what to say to the congregation."

His pastor responded, "At a time like this, we pray the lament psalms. I'm going to prepare for the service. You go hang up black cloths over the windows

---

1. "1989 Tiananmen Square Protests," Wikipedia, last modified 21 December 2020, https://en.wikipedia.org/wiki/1989_Tiananmen_Square_protests.

and walls of the worship hall." Black banners are usually put up as a sign of mourning in a Christian funeral service.

After some time, church members started filling up the hall. The service began. The pastors took turns reading communal laments from the book of Psalms. The congregation read responsively, prayed, and sang of the cross and God's sovereignty. There was no sermon. The lament psalms already expressed their feelings, and the imprecatory verses cried for justice. The people left wordlessly, hugging, wiping away tears, entrusting everything to God.

The death toll from the Tiananmen Square Massacre is unclear, with different reports giving divergent numbers. The incident is still a censored topic in the People's Republic of China. Soldiers were ordered to clean up the bloody debris. Mothers searched for missing or wounded children. Would Psalm 137:9 be appropriate at a time like this? "Happy shall they be who take your little ones and dash them against the rock!"

This verse has been described as "one of the most cruel, vengeful ill-wishes in the Bible."[2] Lewis described it as "devilish," opting to interpret the "babies" allegorically as the beginnings of sinful desires.[3] Unless we are in the shoes of the oppressed who have lost children and family, it is hard to wrap our heads around Psalm 137:9. Even if we have family and friends who have been killed, is it acceptable for Christians to rejoice in the deaths of their enemies' children? This psalm will make sense when we understand that the psalmist was claiming God's promises to vindicate his people against their enemies, and such promises were made on the basis of Zion theology.[4]

Zion Theology

Zion theology is *not* Zionism: the latter is the belief in the political restoration of Israel and is built on dispensational theology, which imposes a literal interpretation on the OT and NT.[5] In contrast, Zion theology is founded on ancient Near Eastern beliefs about the creation of the world. The primaeval

2. Erhard S. Gerstenberger, *Psalms, Part 2, and Lamentations*, FOTL (Grand Rapids: Eerdmans, 2001).

3. Lewis, *Reflections on the Psalms*, 20, 136.

4. Allen, *Psalms 101–150*, 303, and Goldingay, *Psalms*, 3:602, classify Ps 137 as both a lament psalm and a Zion song.

5. Colin Chapman, *Whose Promised Land? The Continuing Crisis over Israel and Palestine* (Grand Rapids: Baker, 2002). Thus, Israel is considered a political entity that is sharply differentiated from the NT church, regardless of the literary and theological contexts of the NT writers.

chaos, usually represented by the sea deity, is defeated in battle by a warrior god, thus establishing order over chaos and paving the way for life to flourish (see ch. 8). The other gods then build a palace for the victor on the highest mountain, where he is enthroned as king.

The Israelites took over this worldview but proclaimed YHWH as the sole and victorious creator of the world. There are obvious similarities and differences between the biblical and ancient Near Eastern perspectives. For example, Genesis 1 presents YHWH as controlling the cosmic and earthly waters without a battle. The establishment of the natural order correlates with social and moral order so that there can be peace and well-being for all.

Zion theology builds on creation theology but focuses on the temple mount where YHWH is enthroned as sovereign king over his people Israel and all nations. Based on past scholarship,[6] the following list is a summary of characteristics of Zion theology that are relevant for our discussion of Psalm 137.

1. YHWH's kingship is based on his role as creator (Pss 93, 29, 89).

2. YHWH's throne is on Mt. Zion, just as the Canaanite god, Baal, was crowned on Mt. Zaphon in the north (Ps 46:5; Isa 2:2).

3. Zion is a holy place (Ps 99:9), and those who dwell on Zion are to respond with trust and obedience (Isa 30:15).

4. YHWH is Israel's defender against the nations. He has delivered them in history (Ps 99), and even though Jerusalem was destroyed by the Babylonians, Zion still functions as a theological symbol of YHWH's universal reign (Ps 74; Isa 60). The eschatological vision of Zion is of YHWH judging the nations to bring about peace (Isa 2:1–4).

Psalm 137 is a response of faith stirred by Zion theology: it laments the enemies' mocking of God's kingship, yet it swears allegiance to Jerusalem, where God is still enthroned, and calls for God to judge the enemies. The following literary analysis will show that the psalm focuses on Zion. It also makes intertextual allusions to prophetic promises in Obadiah, Jeremiah, and Isaiah about the destruction of Babylon, texts which I will explain as arising out of Zion theology.

---

6. Ollenburger, *Zion*; J. J. M. Roberts, *The Bible and the Ancient Near East* (Winona Lake: Eisenbrauns, 2002); Low, *Mother Zion*.

Genre Analysis

It is clear that Psalm 137 refers to the Babylonian exile after the fall of Jerusalem in 587 BC.[7] Psalm 137 can be divided into three parts: in verses 1–4, a "we" group reflects on the past exile in Babylon; in verses 5–6, an "I" swears to remember Jerusalem in the present; and a prayer in verses 7–9 focuses on the enemies.[8] Below is an analysis of the psalm according to the lament genre.[9]

Complaints by "we" (vv. 1–4)
Complaint about selves
¹ By the rivers of Babylon, there we sat,
　　Yea, we wept when we remembered Zion.
Complaint about enemies
² On the willows in its midst we hung our harps,
　　³ For there our captors asked us for words of a song,
　　　and our mockers for joy,
　　　　"Sing us one of the songs of Zion!"
Complaint about God (implied)
⁴ How could we sing the song of YHWH in a foreign land?
Celebration by "I" (two self-curses as vows to praise, vv. 5–6)
⁵ If I forget you, Jerusalem,
　　may my right hand forget.
⁶ May my tongue cling to my palate,
　　if I do not remember you,
　　　if I do not lift up Jerusalem above the head of my joy.
Curse of the enemies (vv. 7–9)
Curse of Edom
⁷ Remember, YHWH, regarding the Edomites the day of Jerusalem,
　　The ones saying, "Tear down, tear down, to its foundations!"

---

7. Goldingay, *Psalms*, 3:601, discusses whether the psalm was written in Babylon during the exile or in Jerusalem after the exile. Most scholars conclude that it is the latter, based on the reference to Babylon as "there" in vv. 1–2, implying that the psalmist is back in Jerusalem. The mention of Edom also points to Jerusalem in the post-exilic period, when the Edomites encroached on Judean land and fomented unrest. Although Babylon fell to the Persians in 539 BC, it was not physically destroyed till centuries later by other conquerors, thus vv. 8–9 wishing for the city's destruction would still make sense after the exile. Both Edom and Babylon became symbols of oppressive powers, even in the time of Ezra and Nehemiah.

8. Hossfeld and Zenger, *Psalms*, 3:513.

9. The translations of Psalm 137 in this chapter are my own.

Curse of Babylon/confidence in God
[8] Daughter Babylon, the devastated,
  commendable are those who will pay you back
    the dealings you dealt to us!
[9] Commendable are those who will seize
  And smash your babies against the crag.

Verse 4 summarizes the exiles' complaints: about the enemies who mocked them by asking them to sing, about themselves being too sad to sing, and even about God who allowed them to be captured. There is no call for help in this lament psalm, except to curse the enemies in verse 7. While verses 8–9 can be considered part of this curse, they are written in the form of commendations of the avenger rather than as requests to God and thus function as statements of confidence that God will act.[10]

The vow to praise usually comes at the end of a lament psalm, but here it is at the centre in verses 5–6, turning the focus on Zion theology. The verses ironically take the form of self-imprecations as oaths never to forget Jerusalem even when the situation is hopeless. Interestingly, only the "I" rather than the "we" vows to remember Jerusalem, implying that the psalmist set the example for his dejected companions. This vow is based on YHWH's kingship in Zion over all the nations and is, therefore, the answer to their past complaints and the foundation for their future restoration.

Poetic Analysis

Complaints (vv. 1–4)
A [1] By ['al] the rivers of **Babylon**, there we sat,
  B Yea, we **wept** when we remembered **Zion**.
    [2] On ['al] the willows in its midst we hung our harps,
      C [3] For there our **captors** asked us for words of a song,
      C' and our **mockers**[11] for joy,
    B' "**Sing** us one of the songs of **Zion**!"
A' [4] How could we sing the song of YHWH in ['al] a **foreign land**?

---

10. Also Goldingay, *Psalms*, 3:601.

11. I follow Goldingay, 3:599, n. 2, who offers some text-critical reasons for translating *tolalenu* as "mockers" rather than "tormentors." It is a *hapax legomenon*, meaning it appears only once in the Hebrew Bible, so its meaning cannot be determined with certainty.

Structurally, verses 1–4 are a chiastic arrangement showing that the exiles are surrounded by Babylon (AA'). There is also the repetition of the preposition 'al (by//in). In the inner circle (BB'), they weep, unable to sing the songs of Zion. The songs may refer to the Zion psalms (e.g. Pss 46, 48, 76, 84),[12] the lyrics of which the captives cannot sing, either because of their pain or to avoid their captors' mocking. The central focus (CC') is on these mockers who challenge their faith in YHWH and Zion theology.

The answer to the taunts can be found in the two overlapping chiasms of the same stanza. The first set is in verses 1–2:

> ¹ *By* ['al] the rivers of Babylon, there we sat,
>> Yea, we wept when we remembered **Zion**.
> ² *On* ['al] the willows in its midst we hung our harps.[13]

The second set is in verses 2–4:

> ² *On* ['al] the willows in its midst we hung our harps,
>> ³ For there our captors asked us for words of a song,
>>> and our mockers for joy,
>>>> "Sing us one of the songs of **Zion**!"
> ⁴ How could we sing the song of YHWH *in* ['al] a foreign land?[14]

The two sets of chiasms begin and end with the preposition 'al (by//on//in). Zion stays at the centre of their struggle.

> *Celebration (vow to praise, vv. 5–6)*
> ⁵ If I forget you, **Jerusalem**,
>> may **my right hand** forget.
> ⁶ May **my tongue** cling to my palate,
>> if I do not remember you,
>> if I do not lift up **Jerusalem** above the head of my joy.

Verses 5–6 also form a chiasm, as shown above.[15] Instead of Babylon, the psalmist now encircles himself by remembering "Jerusalem." At the heart of it, the psalmist swears never to forget the city. For a musician, his hand and tongue

12. Goldingay, 3:604.

13. So also Daniel Simango, "Psalms 137," *Old Testament Exegesis* 31, no. 1 (2018): 222.

14. I have arranged vv. 2–3 as a four-line colon connected by "for" as the reason why they would not sing. It replays the continuous taunting inflicted by the victors on the captives. In contrast, v. 4 ends in a single colon, representing their refusal to sing as they choke on their tears.

15. Simango, "Psalms 137," 225.

would be his most treasured possessions, but they are nothing compared with the joy of Jerusalem.

Jerusalem the city can be used synonymously with Zion the mountain, with both representing the seat of God's protective presence.[16] While Zion symbolizes this theological belief, Jerusalem refers to the city as the nation's political capital. Thus for the psalmist, Zion theology is tied to the physical restoration of Jerusalem.[17] With this hope represented by Jerusalem, the psalmist asks God for vengeance against the enemies.

Curse of the enemies (vv. 7–9)

[7] Remember, YHWH, regarding the Edomites the day of Jerusalem,
> The ones saying, "Tear down, tear down, to its foundations!"

[8] Daughter Babylon [*bath-Bavel*],[18] the devastated [passive of *shadad*]
> Commendable are those who will pay you back [*piel* of *shalem*][19]
> > the dealings [*gemul*] you dealt [*gamal*] to us!

[9] Commendable are those who will seize
> And smash [*piel* of *naphats*][20] your babies [*'olal*] against the crag [*sela'*].

This third stanza continues the theme of "remember," asking God to remember their destroyers. The "day" of Jerusalem (v. 7) is referred to ten times in Obadiah, condemning the Edomites for gloating over Judah's fall.[21] The literary link to Obadiah is another appeal to Zion theology, as indicated in Obadiah 17 and 21:

---

16. Zion and Jerusalem occur seventeen times in the book of Isaiah synonymously.

17. Goldingay, *Psalms*, 3:606.

18. "Daughter Babylon" (*bath-Bavel*) does not mean "daughter of Babylon" but is a personification of the city itself. In ancient West Semitic culture, a city was regarded as a woman who nurtured her people, but it may be called "daughter" to evoke pity for a vulnerable maid (Low, *Mother Zion*, 53–56, 186). The title in Ps 137:8 thus portends Babylon's fall and is so used in Jer 50:42; 51:44; and Isa 47:1 (Goldingay, *Psalms*, 3:609).

19. While *shalem* means "be complete" in the basic *qal* stem, in the intensive *piel* stem, it means "to pay back."

20. The *qal* of *naphats* means "to shatter," while the *piel* stem means "to dash to pieces."

21. Ezek 25:12 and 35:5 also warn that God will act against Edom for welcoming the Babylonian troops and joining them in looting the city.

But on Mount Zion there shall be those that escape,
> and it shall be holy;
>> and the house of Jacob shall take possession of those
>> who dispossessed them.

. . .

Those who have been saved shall go up to Mount Zion
> to rule Mount Esau;
and the kingdom shall be the LORD's.

With the universal rule of God represented by Zion, Israel believe that they will eventually conquer Edom. This promise was ultimately fulfilled paradoxically. After the Maccabean Revolt in 160 BC, Edom, known as Idumea, came under Judean control. The people accepted the Jewish religion, Herod an Idumean ruled Judah, and many Idumeans followed Jesus.[22]

The statements against Babylon in verses 8–9 are written as commendations of the avenger who fulfils God's promises about Babylon's destruction from Jeremiah 50–51 and Isaiah 13 and 47.[23] Below, I highlight the Hebrew words in Jeremiah 51 used in Psalm 137:8–9 (indicated in parentheses in both texts).[24]

⁶ Flee from the midst of Babylon,
> save your lives, each of you!
Do not perish because of her guilt,
> for this is the time of the LORD's vengeance;
>> he is repaying [*shalem*][25] her what is due [*gemul*].

. . .

²⁰ You are my war-club, my weapon of battle:
with you I smash [*naphats*][26] nations;
> with you I destroy kingdoms;
²¹ with you I smash [*naphats*] the horse and its rider;
> with you I smash [*naphats*] the chariot and the
> charioteer;
²² with you I smash [*naphats*] man and woman;
> with you I smash [*naphats*] the old man and the boy;

---

22. Goldingay, *Psalms*, 3:613.

23. Goldingay, 3:608.

24. On the question of whether Ps 137 is earlier or later than the prophetic texts, Goldingay, 3:608, n. 26, notes that it is hard to date all the oracles in Obadiah, Jeremiah, and Isa 13 after the exile.

25. All occurrences of *shalem* in Jer 51 are in the *piel* stem.

26. All occurrences of *naphats* in Jer 51 are in the *piel* stem.

with you I smash [*naphats*] the young man and the girl;
²³ with you I smash [*naphats*] shepherds and their flocks;
with you I smash [*naphats*] farmers and their teams;
with you I smash [*naphats*] governors and deputies.

²⁴ I will repay [*shalem*] Babylon and all the inhabitants of Chaldea before your very eyes for all the wrong that they have done in Zion, says the LORD.

²⁵ I am against you, O destroying mountain,
		says the LORD,
	that destroys the whole earth;
I will stretch out my hand against you,
	and roll you down from the crags [*sela'*],
	and make you a burned-out mountain.
. . .

³³ For thus says the LORD of hosts, the God of Israel:
Daughter Babylon [*bath-Bavel*] is like a threshing-floor
	at the time when it is trodden;
yet a little while
	and the time of her harvest will come.
. . .

⁵⁵ For the LORD is laying Babylon waste [*shadad*],
	and stilling her loud clamour.
Their waves roar like mighty waters,
	the sound of their clamour resounds;
⁵⁶ for a destroyer [*shadad*] has come against her,
	against Babylon;
her warriors are taken,
	their bows are broken;
for the LORD is a God of recompense [*gemul*],
	he will repay in full [*shalem*]. (Jer 51)

In Jeremiah 51, God will devastate Babylon, and because the psalmist is sure that this will take place, he describes Babylon as already "devastated" (the passive of *shadad*) in Psalm 137:8.²⁷ Jeremiah 51:25 refers to a crag or rock

---

27. Hossfeld and Zenger, *Psalms*, 3:512, n. d., discuss the text-critical issue of emending the passive to the active sense of "devastate" to describe Babylon as the oppressor. With most commentators, I believe it is not necessary to emend because the description can be taken as a statement of confidence and faith.

(*sela'*), though in the plural. Some take "crag" to mean the city's foundation, but this does not make sense geographically because Babylon was not built on a rocky place; it is probably a standard concept for powerful cities.[28] "Crag" in Jeremiah 51:25–26 is part of a topographical metaphor with Babylon first as a destroying mountain and then as a burned-out pile. The metaphorical use of "crag" should signal that it is also used figuratively in Psalm 137:9.

The word "smash" (*piel* of *naphats*) is used nine times in Jeremiah 51:20–23 to emphasize the destruction of Babylon's inhabitants. Although "babies" (*'olal*) is not mentioned, Jeremiah 51:22 includes *na'ar* (boy or youth), a word loose enough to include a child (e.g. Exod 2:6). In the light of Jeremiah 51, "babies" in Psalm 137 can be regarded as a synecdoche for Babylon's people. A synecdoche is a figure of speech where one part represents the whole, so here "babies" represents the inhabitants: the military, civilian, economic, and political residents, inclusive of the weakest and youngest members. The use of *'olal* accentuates the population's helplessness.

There is another occurrence of *'olal* in Isaiah's prophecies of judgment against Babylon. Isaiah 13 and 47 describe the destruction of Babylon's children.

> [16] Their infants [*'olal*] will be dashed to pieces[29]
>> before their eyes;
> their houses will be plundered,
>> and their wives ravished.
> [17] See, I am stirring up the Medes against them,
>> who have no regard for silver
>> and do not delight in gold.
> [18] Their bows will slaughter the young men;
>> they will have no mercy on the *fruit of the womb*;
>> their eyes will not pity *children*. (Isa 13)

> [1] Come down and sit in the dust,
>> virgin Daughter Babylon [*bath-Bavel*]!
> . . .
> [8] Now therefore hear this, you lover of pleasures,
>> who sit securely,
> who say in your heart,
>> "I am, and there is no one besides me;

---

28. Gerstenberger, *Psalms, Part 2*, 393.

29. "Dashed to pieces" in Isa 13:16 is from the *piel* of *ratash*, a different word from that in Ps 137:9 but with the same meaning.

I shall not sit as a widow
or know the loss of *children*" –
⁹ both these things shall come upon you
in a moment, in one day:
the loss of *children* and widowhood
shall come upon you in full measure,
in spite of your many sorceries
and the great power of your enchantments. (Isa 47)

In the above texts, words related to 'olal are used – for example, the fruit of the womb and children (italicized above).[30] Smashing babies in Psalm 137 is thus not a vicious fantasy but a vigorous faith in prophetic judgment.

The psalmist declares as 'ashre those who attack Babylon, which I translate as "commendable" rather than the usual "happy." The verbal root 'ashar means to go straight or to set right.[31] It is used mainly in the Psalms and Proverbs to describe the blessed state of those who obey the Torah and fear God.[32] 'Ashre also applies to those who live in Zion (Pss 65:5; 84:5, 6, 13; Isa 30:18–19), so it is appropriate that Psalm 137:8–9 uses it for those who will restore Zion. The descriptor implies that the destroyers are executing justice rather than gleefully committing violence.

Structural Analysis

I present an overall chiastic structure of Psalm 137, with the parallel words highlighted:[33]

A ¹ By the rivers of **Babylon**, there we sat,
B Yea, we wept when we **remembered** Zion . . .
C ⁵ If I forget you, **Jerusalem**,

---

30. Hossfeld and Zenger, *Psalms*, 3:520, suggest that since "children" in Isa 47 refers to the Babylonian dynasty, killing "babies" in Ps 137 means ending Babylon's royal rule. While this interpretation may suit the context of Isa 47, where Babylon is personified as a queen, 'olal in Isa 13 refers to the people of Babylon in general. Thus, Ps 137:9 cannot be justified as a reference only to the royal lineage.

31. C. L. Seow, "An Exquisitely Poetic Introduction to the Psalter," *Journal of Biblical Literature* 132, no. 2 (2013): 277.

32. Henri Cazalles, "אַשְׁרֵי," *TDOT* 1:446–47.

33. D. N. Freedman, *Pottery, Poetry, and Prophecy: Studies in Early Hebrew Poetry* (Winona Lake: Eisenbrauns, 1980), 303–21, has another chiastic model based on grammatical structure that puts vv. 5–6a in the centre. However, Allen, *Psalms 101–150*, 305, critiques it as ignoring the key terms such as "remember" and "Zion," which are highlighted in my model.

> **D** if I do not **remember** you,
> **C'** if I do not lift up **Jerusalem** above the head of my joy.
> **B'** [7] **Remember**, YHWH,
> regarding the Edomites the day of **Jerusalem**,
> **A'** [8] Daughter **Babylon**, the devastated . . .

In AA', "Babylon" begins and ends the chiasm, reflecting both its elevation and end. BB' shows that when people and God "remember Zion/Jerusalem," Babylon's downfall is inevitable. CC' lifts "Jerusalem" up as the focal point of the people's hope for restoration. At the centre, D, the psalmist himself resolutely "remembers" Jerusalem. The chiastic arrangement shows the significance of clinging to Zion, not politically but theologically, because only an omnipotent God can deliver an oppressed people.

Theological Analysis: Zion Theology

Psalm 137's emphasis on Zion theology is clear, first, from its poetic and structural arrangement, and second, from its connections to prophetic texts about the destruction of Israel's enemies.

The poetic focus is seen from the following:

- "Zion" at the centre of two overlapping chiasms in verses 1–4;
- "Jerusalem" at the beginning and end of the chiasm of verses 5–6;
- the chiastic climax of the entire psalm in verses 5–6, where the psalmist swears to remember Jerusalem.

The allusions to other prophetic texts (Obadiah, Jeremiah, and Isaiah) also revolve around Zion. "The day of Jerusalem" in Psalm 137:7 harks back to Obadiah, which prophesied that Mount Zion would rule Mount Esau (Obad 21). The destruction of Daughter Babylon recollects God's promise in Jeremiah 51 to "smash" and "repay" what is "due" by rolling "Daughter Babylon" off the "crags" so that she will be "devastated." That Jeremiah 51 appeals to Zion theology is seen from the following text:[34]

> [10] The LORD has brought forth our vindication;
> come, let us declare in Zion
> the work of the LORD our God.
> [11] Sharpen the arrows!
> Fill the quivers!

---

34. While Jeremiah's theology is Deuteronomic in terms of God's punishment against Israel, the hope of restoration is linked to Zion (Jer 3:14; 30:17; 31:6, 12; 50:5, 28; 51:10, 24, 35).

The LORD has stirred up the spirit of the kings of the Medes,
because his purpose concerning Babylon is to destroy it, for
that is the vengeance of the LORD, vengeance for his temple. . . .

[15] It is he who made the earth by his power,
   who established the world by his wisdom,
and by his understanding stretched out the heavens.
[16] When he utters his voice there is a tumult of waters in the
   heavens,
   and he makes the mist rise from the ends of the earth.
He makes lightnings for the rain,
   and he brings out the wind from his storehouses.

(51:10–11, 15–16)

Zion is mentioned in Jeremiah 51:10–11, where God is the avenging warrior.
The temple in verse 11 is where God is enthroned. He is also described as the
creator in verses 15–16, which is the basis for his universal rule. As YHWH is
the ruler, Jeremiah 51:6 and 56 state that YHWH will "repay" (piel of shalem)
Babylon her "due" (gemul), two words also used in Psalm 137:8.[35]

What were the Babylonians' "dealings" (gemul) with Jerusalem? When
Zedekiah, the last Judean king, rebelled, Nebuchadnezzar of Babylon besieged
Jerusalem, resulting in a severe famine in the city (2 Kgs 25:1–4). Both the
Bible and other ancient records write about hunger driving men and women
to eat their children's flesh. It was also common in battles to rip open pregnant
women and kill infants.[36] Psalm 137 is, therefore, asking for justice that befits
the crime.

Although it seems unfair that innocent children should suffer,[37] in chapter
4 I referred to the concept of "ruler punishment" proposed by Daube. He
explains it as "where the wrong committed by a ruler is repaid to him by a move
against those under his rule, by taking away or damaging his free subjects."[38]
In other words, the king's subjects suffer the terrible consequences of his sin.

---

35. Hossfeld and Zenger, Psalms, 3:519, explain that "to pay back" (piel of shalem) is a
technical term for retaliation. It is a term that is never used for human retribution but only for
God's revenge.

36. Day, Crying for Justice, 65. See 2 Kgs 8:12; 15:16.

37. Day, 71, defends God's right to punish the children for the fathers' iniquity based
on Exod 34:7. "God has rights that man cannot have, for only he is God. Harsh and revolting
though his justice may appear, the believer is called to trust God's goodness, even in the midst
of his justice, and accept any concomitant tensions." However, I propose "ruler punishment"
as a more helpful concept.

38. Daube, Studies in Biblical Law, 163.

A modern-day example would be the atomic bombings of Hiroshima and Nagasaki in order to bring an end to World War II. These were horrifying events that should be considered with much sorrow by both the victims and the victors.

The idea of "ruler punishment" is reflected in Isaiah 14:21–22 regarding the downfall of the king of Babylon:

> [21] Prepare slaughter for his sons
>   because of the guilt of their father.
> Let them never rise to possess the earth
>   or cover the face of the world with cities.
>
> [22] I will rise up against them, says the LORD of hosts, and will cut off from Babylon name and remnant, offspring and posterity, says the LORD.

Isaiah 14:22 is the conclusion to oracles of judgment against Babylon in Isaiah 13 and its king in Isaiah 14. Such punishment rests on Zion theology, as indicated in Isaiah 14:13, where the Babylonian monarch makes the following boast:

> You said in your heart,
>   "I will ascend to heaven;
> I will raise my throne
>   above the stars of God;
> I will sit on the mount of assembly
>   on the heights of Zaphon."

Zaphon, meaning "north," refers in the ancient Near Eastern context to the mythical mountain where the king of gods dwells. In the Israelite context, it is identified with Mt. Zion (Ps 48:2). YHWH, the true sovereign, will judge the earthly king and send him to Sheol for his arrogance.

Zion theology continues as an important theme in the NT, especially in the gospels and the Epistle to the Hebrews.[39] The NT people of God are said to "have come to Mount Zion and to the city of the living God, the heavenly Jerusalem" (Heb 12:22). We, too, await the heavenly Jerusalem, which is glorified in Revelation 21. Thus, we may pray Psalm 137 with confidence that God will establish his righteous reign over the chaos of human atrocities.

---

39. Kiwoong Son, *Zion Symbolism in Hebrews: Hebrews 12:18–24 as a Hermeneutical Key to the Epistle*, Paternoster Biblical Monographs (Milton Keynes: Paternoster, 2005); Kim Huat Tan, *The Zion Traditions and the Aims of Jesus*, SNTSMS 91 (Cambridge: Cambridge University Press, 1997).

Conclusion

Modern wars are as horrific as ancient ones, and Psalm 137 is still relevant in beseeching God as the universal ruler for just retribution. During World War II, Nazis invaded Poland, pierced children on pitchforks, and threw them onto the smouldering coals of the barn where their parents had been burned to death.[40] Similar carnage was happening in Asia at the same time. During the Rape of Nanjing in 1937, Japanese soldiers searched from door to door for girls to abuse. Most women were killed immediately after being raped, often through mutilation or penetrating vaginas with bayonets, long bamboo sticks, or other objects. Genitals of children were cut open so that the soldiers could rape them. Babies were bayonetted.[41] Would the victims think that Psalm 137 was "devilish" or desirable?

With regard to more recent history, Brueggemann wrote in 1984 that this psalm "could serve a Catholic in Northern Ireland, a black in South Africa, a Palestinian on the West Bank, and exploited women in our society."[42] As I write this chapter in 2021, this psalm could also serve Syrian refugees, victims of terrorist bombings, Rohingyas in Bangladesh, Afghans under the Taliban, and Burmese protestors under the military junta. A former student of mine, who is from the Karen tribe in Myanmar, penned the imprecatory psalm below in the spirit of Psalm 137 regarding atrocities committed by the army against its own people.

> Where is your justice?
> Where is your vengeance against these rabid dogs?
> The enemies robbed us not only of our livelihoods, our lands,
> and our limbs,
> but they tore away our husbands from our embrace,
> our nursing children from our bosoms,
> and our hopes for a peaceful home of our own.
> LORD, do you not see them plotting evil after evil?
> Do you not hear the terrors of children being burned
> alive?
> Do you not smell our desperation?

40. Athalya Brenner, "On the Rivers of Babylon (Psalm 137), or Between Victim and Perpetrator," in *Sanctified Aggression*, eds. Jonneke Bekkenkamp and Yvonne Sherwood (London: T&T Clark, 2003), 76–91, cited in Goldingay, *Psalms*, 3:611.

41. "Nanjing Massacre," Wikipedia, last modified 13 December 2020, https://en.wikipedia.org/wiki/Nanjing_Massacre.

42. Brueggemann, *Message of the Psalms*, 75.

I know you hear;
    I know you see;
        Your arms are not too short to save.
LORD, when they send their planes to attack unarmed villagers,
    let the planes run amok into mountainsides!
When they send their guns to shoot villagers working in their
  fields,
    let their eyes be blinded and minds confused
        so that they turn on one another!
When they plot evil against your children,
    let their children bear the consequences of their evil!
LORD, do not delay,
    Do not deny us this we pray.
        We trust in your justice till the end of days![43]

43. Naw Winsome Paul, unpublished work, used by permission of author.

11

Ministering with the Psalms of Vengeance

This chapter provides a step-by-step guide to working through anger and other emotional issues. I address the counsellor in this chapter, but individuals can also go through the steps on their own. I use the lament psalms as a model for ministering in prayer. As stated in chapter 8, the lament genre has the following elements:

- Complaints (about God, self, and enemy)
- Call to God for help
- Confession of sin or contention of innocence
- Curse of enemies
- Confidence in God
- Celebration (vow of thanksgiving)

My prayer model has five main parts based on the above elements:

I. Complain
   1. Complain by the counsellee
   2. Confidence in God prayed by the counsellor
II. Commit
   1. Understand the offender
      a. If there is repentance, forgive
      b. If there is no repentance, give justice to God
   2. Bless the offender
III. Confess
   1. Confession by the counsellee
   2. Confidence in God by the counsellor
IV. Call for help
   – by the counsellor

V. Celebrate
1. Celebration by the counsellee
2. Celebration by the counsellor

The imprecatory psalms are particularly relevant at II.1.b: if there is no repentance, give justice to God. Before the prayer ministry, the counsellor should have interviewed the counsellee to ascertain the roots of the problem as far as possible. Equip yourself with some good books on counselling.[1] Depression is often a sign of anger, particularly when one has not been allowed to express negative feelings. Explore significant relationships and past events that may have impacted the counsellee. Explain the steps in the prayer that you will be guiding him or her through. Begin with an opening prayer, acknowledging God's presence and the Spirit's guidance.

I. Complain

1. Complain by the Counsellee

Just as the psalmist complains by pouring out his struggles to God, so this is the first step for the counsellee. Ask the Spirit to bring whatever he wants to deal with to the counsellee's mind. Then invite the counsellee to talk to God about the past incidents and how he or she felt. Sometimes, a counsellee is unable to express his or her emotions for the following reasons, and the counsellor will need to address the blockage.

a. Emotions Are Unbiblical

Many counsellees begin with forgiving the wrongdoer because the Christian assumption that anger is wrong may be deeply ingrained. Stop them gently. Explain that unresolved emotions fester like pus in a wound. To heal the infection, a doctor has to remove the pus and clean it up. Ignoring feelings and going straight to forgiveness is like sticking a Band-Aid on a festering sore, fooling us into thinking that we are OK even as the infection spreads throughout our body.

While conversing with a young woman, I casually asked about her parents. She told me that her mother had passed away many years ago when she was a teenager. I inquired whether she had died of an illness. "No, she was murdered," she answered unemotionally. Shocked, I responded by saying that she must

---

1. E.g. Gary R. Collins, *Christian Counselling: A Comprehensive Guide*, 3rd ed. (Nashville: Thomas Nelson, 2007).

have had a hard time over this tragedy. After a few silent moments, tears rolled down, and she told me that this was the first time she had wept over her mother.

At her mother's funeral, pastors and church members had comforted her by telling her not to cry because God must have a good purpose, and she should forgive the murderer. So, she had held back her tears all these years, but the pain was still palpable. I told her Jesus wept when his friend Lazarus died (John 11:35). Our trauma cannot be dealt with if we repress our emotions.

b. Emotions Are Unspeakable

Some experiences may be too painful to describe out loud, especially when the victims feel that they have been shamed. When they can't pray, offer to pray on their behalf. It will give them the voice and vocabulary to acknowledge their own anguish before God.

Junie shared with me about being sexually assaulted as a child whenever the family visited her uncle. He would take her to a room while her parents were occupied, and they never found out what happened. I invited her to pray about the past incidents, but she could only shut her eyes tight and clench her fists. After some time, I offered to pray for her, and she nodded. I said that we hated the uncle for what he had done, and asked how God could have allowed such a thing to happen. As I went on, tears started streaming down her face, and then she added her own cries, asking why her parents didn't care enough to find out what happened. The counsellor may need to prime the pump of the emotional well before the water can gush out.

c. Emotions Are Inaccessible

Some cannot get in touch with their memories and feelings because they are deeply repressed. Helping the counsellee will require peeling the onion, starting with whatever he or she can recall. As we deal with each layer, the counsellee may remember earlier incidents.[2]

---

2. Some counsellors include prenatal memories, i.e. memories while still in the womb. Charles Kraft, *Deep Wounds, Deep Healing: Discovering the Vital Link between Spiritual Warfare and Inner Healing* (Ann Arbor: Servant Publications, 1993), 114–17, writes that a foetus may be affected by the feelings and traumas of the mother through their biological connection. Emotion produces biochemicals, which are transmitted through the bloodstream. Such experiences are imprinted in the developing brain cells of the foetus and become part of its subconscious memory. However, I recommend that any suspected problems at the prenatal stage, whether maternal rejection or an attempted abortion, should be corroborated lest they be false memories. For instance, a young man was told that he had anxiety because when his mother was pregnant with him and his twin brother, she was worried about supporting both of them. This young man went back and asked his mum about it, but she said that both she and his father were overjoyed

Millie felt that she was never good enough, saying that her father always expected her to do better. Her last conversation with her father ended in grief. He was working overseas, and when she told him of her school results over the phone, he said to her, "You are a disgrace!" Those were the last words she heard – her father died soon after from a heart attack. Her anguish and self-recriminations were still raw, so we worked through that last conversation first.

Millie had a sense of relief but still struggled with self-doubt. As we continued to meet and talk, she recalled that she had won a prize in preschool, but it was a sad occasion for her. While all the other children came to the award ceremony with their parents, hers did not turn up. Her father was busy at work, while her mother had to look after her baby sister. She felt overlooked and insignificant. We brought this childhood memory to God in prayer, affirming that God would have rejoiced over her.

d. Emotions Are Unacceptable

Some people are uncomfortable voicing anger about their parents; for example, it would be considered unfilial for Asians. Trixie was troubled by her quick temper, which we realized was a defensive reaction to her mother. She was an unwanted pregnancy to her mum, but her father insisted on keeping her. As she grew up, her mother often berated her for her physical appearance and caned her for minor matters. However, during our time of prayer, Trixie was hesitant to express her rage against her mother.

I assured her that emotions are not wrong – it depends what we do with them. Besides, parents are not perfect, and they can hurt us. Some may have good intentions but make mistakes; others, sadly, have wrong motives that they need to be convicted of. The Bible is realistic about this. Psalm 27:10 says, "If my father and mother forsake me, the LORD will take me up." God knows that human parents are imperfect when he says in Isaiah 49:15,

> Can a woman forget her nursing-child,
>> or show no compassion for the child of her womb?
> Even these may forget,
>> yet I will not forget you.

A human mother may lack compassion for her child, but God says he is the only perfect mother. Expressing our feelings about our parents shows that we recognize that what they did was unacceptable so that we will not repeat it

---

to have twins. On the other hand, when a mother has attempted abortion or carried the child despite not wanting it, there are likely to be some emotional effects.

ourselves. As we resolve our hurt and anger, we can move towards honouring them with the right attitude of grace and respect. Eventually, Trixie poured out to God her feelings of hatred towards her mother and, over time, felt the chains of her own anger loosened.

In the process, Trixie asked why God had allowed her to be born into such a family. The counsellor does not need to be taken aback by this, and in fact, it is helpful to ask if the person harbours resentment against God for letting bad things happen to him or her. Some counsellees may be reticent because they have been taught that one is not allowed to question God.

Explain that God values authenticity rather than false spirituality. Only then can one encounter God and hear his response even in the depths of our despondency. Psalm 22:1–2 is a good example:

> My God, my God, why have you forsaken me?
> > Why are you so far from helping me, from the words of
> > my groaning?
> O my God, I cry by day, but you do not answer;
> > and by night, but find no rest.

The pray-er is accusing God of not caring, not listening, and not answering. Jesus himself echoed the first line of this psalm while on the cross.

If we think that Psalm 22 is merely a cry of desperation rather than anger, then there is the example of Job. He suffered the destruction of his property, the deaths of all his ten children, and a miserable disease. It was only when his wife challenged him to live up to his integrity that he finally ventilated to God about the injustice inflicted upon him. In response, God let him go on arguing before answering in the thirty-eighth chapter of the book of Job. In the epilogue, God commended Job for speaking rightly *to*[3] God, while his friends had failed to do so (Job 42:7–8). Only Job talked to God, even if it was to accuse God of being a tyrant, while his friends only lectured about God. In the end, God restored Job but reprimanded his friends.

Some practitioners counsel people to forgive God, that is, to release all anger towards God for allowing hurtful events to happen.[4] This view may be "good" psychology but it is bad theology, because it implies that God has sinned against us. Job did not forgive God; instead, he came to a deeper understanding of God's sovereign wisdom, though he never understood why

---

3. The English versions have "spoken *about* me," but C. L. Seow, *Job 1–21: Interpretation and Commentary*, Illuminations (Grand Rapids: Eerdmans, 2013), 92, points out that the Hebrew text is literally "spoken to [ʾel] me."

4. Kraft, *Deep Wounds, Deep Healing*, 122.

God did what he did. In the same way, help the counsellee by pointing to the truths of God's character.

2. Confidence in God by the Counsellor

In a lament psalm, the psalmist will come to a point where he turns to God in faith. This is the statement of "Confidence in God." One can affirm one's faith for oneself, but the counsellor can give more assurance of God's presence and comfort.

Consolation is best found in the incarnated Christ, who understands us perfectly.[5] Hebrews 4:15 says, "For we do not have a high priest who is unable to sympathize with our weaknesses, but we have one who in every respect has been tested as we are, yet without sin." So whatever the counsellee has gone through, Jesus understands better than anyone else because he has undergone the same affliction more profoundly. He empathizes with every tear and cry because "in the days of his flesh, Jesus offered up prayers and supplications, with loud cries and tears, to the one who was able to save him from death, and he was heard because of his reverent submission" (Heb 5:7).

For Junie, who was sexually abused, Jesus knew what physical abuse was when he was slapped by the Roman soldiers, whipped by lashes, nailed to the cross, and stripped naked. When she felt that her parents didn't care, Jesus's family didn't understand him either, thinking that he was mad (Mark 3:21). His disciples betrayed him and fled, and his heavenly Father abandoned him. Although the situations may not be exactly parallel, Jesus has experienced the same agony, even to the point of death.

For Chrissie, whose mother accused her of lying about being molested by her brother, Jesus also knew what it is like to be falsely accused. Despite coming to save the world, he was rejected by his own people, slandered for doing good, called a blasphemer, and labelled a criminal. He experienced injustice and trusted God for vindication.

Abel was struggling with his studies when he came to see me. He told me about a teacher in primary school who put him down with the words, "You will end up as a rubbish collector!" During our time of prayer, he was comforted knowing that he was in good company because Jesus also had insults thrown

---

5. Dennis Linn and Matthew Linn, *Healing Life's Hurts: Healing Memories through the Five Stages of Forgiveness* (New York: Paulist Press, 1978), 85. In dealing with each emotion, the authors ask the counsellee to listen to how Christ feels through Scripture and then to live out Christ's reaction.

at him: "Can anything good come out of Nazareth?" (John 1:46); "Is not this the carpenter's son?" (Matt 13:55). They even spat in his face (Matt 26:67). Jesus is on the side of the despised.

I prayed for Julia, a pretty young lady who never thought she was good-looking because her father used to compare her unfavourably with her cousins, who looked like models. In comparison, she felt like an ugly duckling, so she became an academic overachiever to gain her father's affirmation. Jesus, too, "had no form or majesty that we should look at him, nothing in his appearance that we should desire him" (Isa 53:2). More importantly, God looks at the heart and not at the outward appearance (1 Sam 16:7).

Ask God to show you the appropriate biblical example to use. Jesus promised the Holy Spirit in John 14:16–17: "And I will ask the Father, and he will give you another Advocate, to be with you for ever. This is the Spirit of truth." "Advocate" in Greek is *parakalē*, which means literally "one who calls beside," meaning that the Spirit walks beside us and calls to us with words of encouragement. Thus, *parakalē* is also translated as "Comforter" or "Counsellor." As we rely on the Spirit, he will use his truths to minister to the counsellee.

The second step of the prayer ministry is to help the counsellee commit his or her struggles to God.

II. Commit

One commits the problem to God either by forgiving the offender if the person has shown repentance, or, in the absence of repentance, leaving vengeance to God. In either case, the counsellor invites the counsellee to bless the person who hurt him or her as an act of love. In order to pray for the wrongdoer, it helps to understand why the person acted the way he or she did.

1. Understand the Offender

As Volf writes, recognizing our common humanity with those who hurt us helps us manage our outrage.[6] Ephesians 4:31–32 tells us to put away malicious anger and be compassionate to one another. To help the counsellee understand the offender, I would ask during the interview, "Why do you think he (or she) behaves that way? What is it about his family background that makes him the way he is?" This is not making excuses for the other person.

---

6. Volf, *Exclusion and Embrace*, 29.

He is still responsible for the wrongs committed, but it helps the victim be more objective in his or her reactions. At the very least, it provides insights into what to pray for the wrongdoer.[7]

a. If There Is Repentance, Forgive

Yvette was caned weekly by her mother for all sorts of reasons: not doing well in her studies, not paying attention in class, or not practising the piano. During an altercation with her mum, Yvette blurted out a long-harboured thought, "Am I really your daughter?" These words startled her mum, who apologized for being harsh. Her mother tried to change but was not completely successful. She continued to complain at Yvette, making it hard for her to forgive her mum for all the hurts.

When I asked about her mum's background, I learned that Yvette's mum never finished school because she grew up poor. She had wanted piano lessons but never got the opportunity. We can see why she pressured her daughter in her studies and piano playing. Yvette then learned to pray that her mother would be fulfilled in God's love and not through her daughter's achievements. This insight didn't immediately remove Yvette's pain, but it helped her work towards forgiveness.

Asian parents find it hard to verbalize their apologies but may show them by their actions, for example, preparing an extra-nice meal. One could accept that as an acted apology. Parents may have good intentions in disciplining their children to study harder, but they may use the wrong method because they do not know any better. Instead of understanding and affirming, parents may use corporal punishment, assuming that poor grades are always due to laziness. Some counsellees may see their parents' positive intentions demonstrated in other ways, such as making time or financial sacrifices for them. In such situations, it may be appropriate to pray like Jesus, "Father, forgive them, for they know not what they do." I let the counsellee decide on his or her response, as there are parents who are simply abusive and narcissistic.

Guide the counsellee to be specific in prayer so that the counsellee knows he or she has dealt with the issue. Rather than a general "I forgive the person," it is helpful to name the person and what he or she did. Doing so enables the counsellee to accept what happened and intentionally cancel the debt owed. When people find it hard to forgive, they may not have fully expressed their

---

7. I would add a caveat that though it is generally helpful to understand the offender, it may not always be possible or the best place to start, especially in horrifying crimes like rape.

hurt and anger, which may take time. In the meantime, the counsellee can be encouraged to pray, "Help me to forgive," while working through the process.

b. If There Is No Repentance, Give Justice to God

Jack felt cheated by his boss. He and his colleagues were told that they would be given a higher commission if they hit a certain quota in their sales. Jack worked hard because the money would be useful for his new baby. He reached the target, but the boss reneged on his promise, instead promising to pay them later. Months passed, and then the boss denied making the promise but said it was only a possibility. Jack and his colleagues tried to reason with the boss, but he refused to budge.

Jack was furious, so I suggested that we pray using Psalm 109, asking God to execute *lex talionis* on the unscrupulous boss and take away his ill-gotten gains. We prayed that the exploiter be held accountable by God, who is the ultimate boss and judge. Jack left the matter with God and resigned from the company. Some years later, he found out that the firm had gone out of business. Justice was done in Jack's case, but even if we do not get to see it, we can trust that God will eventually carry it out.

Most people are not used to praying the imprecatory psalms, and the counsellor can provide guidance. Read through a psalm with the counsellee, explaining it along the way, and focus on what is especially relevant. Regarding *lex talionis*, one can pray according to the wrong suffered – for example, that God will hold the accuser accountable for every false word, that the abuser will suffer the pain and shame he inflicted, or that the fraudster will lose his fortune. If unsure of what to pray, ask that God will give the enemy what he or she deserves. After all, God will curse the one who curses his people. However, as in Psalm 83, one can also pray for the offender's remorse because that is part of blessing the enemy.

2. Bless the Offender

Invite the counsellee to bless the offender, irrespective of whether he or she has repented or not, because love is unconditional. We do it because it is a command, and doing so helps us grow in the likeness of God. Matthew 5:44–45 says, "But I say to you, Love your enemies and pray for those who persecute you, so that you may be children of your Father in heaven." The more we are like God, the less we feel like victims and are able to see the other person's neediness. What he or she truly needs may not be material health and wealth but to see the truth about God.

Leila was easily triggered by demanding people because her mother was very controlling. Among other things, her mum imposed an early curfew when Leila was young and would embarrass her by yelling at her in front of her bewildered friends. As we talked, Leila realized that her mother had many insecurities from her family background. She had to leave school and look after her younger siblings when she was barely old enough to do so. She was constantly afraid that something unfortunate would happen to her family, so she always tried to control everything, including Leila's life.

Rather than thinking that her mother loved her only if she behaved, Leila recognized that her mum's overprotectiveness was due to her fears. When I asked Leila to pray for her mother, she realized that her mother needed God's security and peace above all else.

III. Confess

There is either a contention of innocence or a confession of sin in the lament psalms. Because both parties may contribute to a conflict, the counsellee needs to reflect on his or her role in the problem. The counsellee may be an innocent victim, but even so, he or she may have reacted inappropriately out of anger and so should be given the opportunity to reflect on this step.

1. Confession by the Counsellee

Ask the Spirit to show the counsellee if there is anything he or she needs to repent of. There may be something the counsellor is unaware of, such as the counsellee harbouring hatred or refusing to help the person hated. Sometimes, the problem may be more subtle, especially when the victim has bought into the lies of his or her past experiences. For example, Leila thought that her mother loved her only if she obeyed her every instruction, so she assumed that God's love was also conditional, which caused her much stress in her ministry. Leila realized that she had limited God's love, and confessed that she had trusted in herself rather than in God.

However, be careful to distinguish a legitimate confession from false guilt. Paul warns about this in 2 Corinthians 7:10: "For godly grief produces a repentance that leads to salvation and brings no regret, but worldly grief produces death." An overly sensitive conscience could cause a counsellee to repent for what is merely a social rather than a moral expectation. For instance, in an environment that emphasizes academic success, students may feel they have failed God when they don't do well. I would ask them what they think

God is looking for at the end of their lives: it would not be their results but whether they have served in faithfulness and love.

For some young people, the lack of parental acceptance has driven them to find love in the wrong places – pornography, premarital sex, or even same-sex relationships. Just as forgiveness needs to be specific, so also does a confession. Lead the counsellee to tell God what he or she did wrong and with whom so that the counsellee can leave all his or her guilt and regrets at the cross of Jesus.

2. Confidence in God by the Counsellor

After the confession, the counsellor assures the counsellee of God's forgiveness. This is another aspect of "Confidence in God" in the lament psalms. For instance, after the psalmist confessed in Psalm 51 (attributed to David after his adultery with Bathsheba and the murder of her husband), he said confidently to God, "Purge me with hyssop, and I shall be clean; wash me, and I shall be whiter than snow" (Ps 51:7).

The counsellor can claim various Scripture texts; for example, 1 John 1:9: "If we confess our sins, he who is faithful and just will forgive us our sins and cleanse us from all unrighteousness." To counteract any sense of false guilt or self-blame, refer to 1 John 2:1–2: "But if anyone does sin, we have an advocate with the Father, Jesus Christ the righteous; and he is the atoning sacrifice for our sins, and not for ours only but also for the sins of the whole world."

Occasionally, some feel that their sin is so heinous that it cannot be forgiven. Jill came to talk to me some time after she had had an abortion. She and her boyfriend had premarital sex, and since they weren't ready to be married, she aborted the baby. She asked, "Will God forgive me?" I pointed her to the story of King David and assured her that God would forgive. However, she was still weighed down by guilt because she couldn't forgive herself.

To believe that God forgives but still be unable to forgive oneself is theologically inconsistent. It means that we think that our sin is too terrible for Jesus to atone for and it sets us up as a judge greater than God. The counsellee needs to affirm by faith that Christ's blood cleanses us from *all* sins and that if the Son has set us free, we are free indeed (John 8:36). Romans 8:33 is also relevant: "Who will bring any charge against God's elect? It is God who justifies." Therefore, God's forgiveness is a truth that needs to be claimed by faith through thanksgiving, despite any subjective feelings to the contrary. Jill eventually rejected the chains of false guilt and found peace in the truth of God's gracious pardon.

IV. Call for Help

After the counsellee has forgiven or committed justice to God and confessed his or her wrongdoings, the counsellor can ask God for healing, just like the "Call for Help" component of a lament psalm. Ask the Holy Spirit to show you the relevant petitions to make according to the counsellee's needs. I give a few examples below.

For Julia, who thought her father considered her ugly, and for Abel, who was called a "rubbish collector" by his teacher, we prayed that they would know how precious they are in God's sight. Psalm 139 is a go-to reference, especially where it says that we are fearfully and wonderfully made (Ps 139:3–4). As for our future, the psalm assures us that God has written down all the days that were formed for us (Ps 139:16).

For those who are fearful, we can pray 1 John 4:18: "perfect love casts out fear." Leila thought love was conditional on her good behaviour, so she became anxious when in her ministry. She needed to know that God's love is already complete and that he sees her heart, not the outcome. God is also the one who enables us, as 2 Timothy 1:6–7 says: "God did not give us a spirit of cowardice, but rather a spirit of power and of love and of self-discipline."

Trixie and Yvette were severely disciplined by their parents physically and verbally. They needed a deep assurance of their worth, rooted in God's perfect fatherly and motherly love. Even if the harsh treatment were dispensed by only one parent, the other parent is seen as complicit in not protecting the child. God's motherly love was mentioned in Isaiah 49:15. God's fatherly love is found in Romans 8:15: "You have received a spirit of adoption. . . . We cry, 'Abba! Father!'" This is a love that "has been poured into our hearts through the Holy Spirit that has been given to us" (Rom 5:5). We can also pray that the counsellees might "have the power to comprehend, with all the saints, what is the breadth and length and height and depth, and to know the love of Christ that surpasses knowledge, so that [they] may be filled with all the fullness of God" (Eph 3:18–19).

Some felt unwanted as children, either because they were unplanned babies or were fostered out because their parents were not financially or emotionally able to bring them up. Candice was made to do all the housework by her uncle, whom she was sent to live with. The uncle would always find fault with her, and her cousins would bully her. She found it healing to know that Jesus especially welcomed the little children and delighted in blessing them, for to such belongs the kingdom of God (Luke 18:15–17).

At times, one might encounter a need for spiritual deliverance if the counsellee has been involved in the occult or if a sin has been deeply entrenched, especially one of a sexual nature. Such sins very easily cause us to lose self-control and come under the influence of the tempter. After I prayed for a young man regarding his addiction to pornography, he shared that he felt suffocated that night by a malevolent presence in his bedroom. He told me that he had always been sceptical of such phenomena, and if he had not experienced it for himself, he would not have believed it.

We do not have space to deal with deliverance or exorcism in this book, but I will share some relevant scriptures that I used to pray with the counsellee. I encouraged him to affirm Christ's lordship and victory against the evil one, using texts such as Philippians 2:9–11; 1 John 4:4; and Colossians 2:15. We have the protection of God (1 John 5:18) and his armour (Eph 6). Singing worship songs is also a helpful way to focus on God. The second night, the young man reported that he slept peacefully and had no unwanted encounters. Whatever the problem may be, Jesus came to fulfil what was promised in Isaiah 61:1: "to bring good news to the oppressed, to bind up the broken-hearted, to proclaim liberty to the captives, and release to the prisoners."

V. Celebrate

Finally, we come to the fifth and last phase of the prayer. Like the lament psalms, we also end with "Celebration," which expresses hope in God's answer. In the OT, the psalmist may vow that he will bring a sacrifice of thanksgiving for God's deliverance. So also, invite the counsellee to offer his or her thanksgiving.

1. Celebration by the Counsellee

The act of thanksgiving can be likened to the counselling technique of reframing an issue or memory. Rather than being stuck with a negative experience, thanksgiving helps the counsellee see that God is still sovereign and can redeem the past. First Thessalonians 5:18 tells us to keep on giving thanks *in* all circumstances. We do not thank God *for* the bad things but for his presence and help in all situations. Ask the counsellee to give thanks for any good that he or she can see coming out of the trials.

Some may acknowledge that it was through the difficulties that they turned to God. As James said, "whenever you face trials of any kind, consider it nothing but joy, because you know that the testing of your faith produces endurance; and let endurance have its full effect, so that you may be mature and complete, lacking in nothing" (1:2–4). In a previous chapter, I shared about my ministry conflict and how it had affected me. When I reflected on what I could give thanks for, I realized that my motivation was refined. Despite thoughts of giving up, I kept going to work day after day, not for the ministry or the people, but because of God's calling.

Others may realize that God can use their experience to comfort those going through the same travail. Second Corinthians 1:3–4 tells us that God consoles us in our afflictions "so that we may be able to console those who are in any affliction with the consolation with which we ourselves are consoled by God." After Millie, whose father had called her a disgrace, worked through her sense of rejection, she developed a passion to set up a ministry to counsel other women.

2. Celebration by the Counsellor

The counsellor prays for the future, thanking God that he will continue to be with the counsellee in the face of daily challenges. For example, if doubts return, pray that the Spirit will keep the counsellee's mind on God's truth (John 14:17). If the counsellee becomes anxious, pray that "the peace of God, which surpasses all understanding," will guard his or her heart and mind in Christ Jesus (Phil 4:6–7).

After the prayer, ask the counsellee how he or she feels and how God has spoken. Many experience peace, relief, joy, or a sense of confidence, and you can usually see the change in their faces. Some may share a picture or a word of assurance that came to their mind. The counsellor can clarify doubts and affirm what was edifying. Because we have asked by faith that the Spirit will minister to the counsellee, we can trust that he will work appropriately in the counsellee's heart and mind.

The prayer session may be a breakthrough, but it is only the first step towards healing. Growth and sanctification are a continuing process, so plan the follow-up. Recommend books that will equip the counsellee with more knowledge and skills to handle his or her issues.[8] Spiritual disciplines will sustain the counsellee's growth; for example, help the counsellee nurture a habit of giving thanks. Thanksgiving is an antidote to anxiety and depression. A good goal would be to write down ten items for thanksgiving every day, but

---

8. I usually recommend Neil T. Anderson, *Victory over Darkness: Realize the Power of Your Identity in Christ*, rev. and updated ed. (Minneapolis: Bethany House, 2000) and *Who I Am in Christ: A Devotional* (Minneapolis: Bethany House, 1993) to build up the biblical foundations of one's identity in Christ. Henry Cloud and John Townsend, *Boundaries: When to Say Yes, When to Say No to Take Control of Your Life*, updated and expanded ed. (Grand Rapids: Zondervan, 2017) and its series are helpful for building healthy relationships.

start with what the counsellee finds doable, for example, three items a day, and then gradually increase it. There can be various categories of gratitude, each day focusing on different aspects, such as the person of God, friends, nature, and so on. If a day is missed, the counsellee shouldn't stop – just continue till the habit becomes second nature.

Encourage the counsellee to find support with trusted friends. In fact, I prefer people to bring a friend along who can support them in the follow-up. Accountability is indispensable when dealing with serious addictive sins, such as pornography. For such issues, plan preventive steps – for example, blocking out porn sites, calling a friend for prayer when one feels tempted, or engaging in a more fulfilling activity.

Where there is a conflict, help counsellees work on reconciliation. They may need guidance on how to communicate in a clear, non-accusatory way. While we must be prepared for the other party not to respond positively, we are accountable to do what God requires of us.

Conclusion

The above five sections were written in a counselling context, but you can also follow the steps on your own. The parts that the counsellor prays are based on scriptural truths about Christ's comfort and his promise of forgiveness, healing, and deliverance. Ultimately, we want counsellees to pray for themselves when encountering difficulties, and to be able to help others as well.

For counsellors, the above process could be done in one session, especially when dealing with a single issue, but the counsellor needs to be flexible. It may be that the background is so complex that the interview and the prayer have to be conducted separately. Sometimes, the counsellee is unable to proceed with forgiveness and needs more time to express his or her struggles. Follow God's timing as he works in the counsellee's life.

I want to leave you with a few spiritual encounters that various people had after the prayer. Candice, who was bullied by her uncle and his family when she was sent to live with them, saw herself as a little girl happily jumping up and down while a giant eagle was flying overhead. She knew that the eagle was God. Though she didn't realize it at that time, this is what God said to the children of Israel in Exodus 19:4: "You have seen what I did to the Egyptians, and how I bore you on eagles' wings and brought you to myself." Candice can be sure that God has rescued her from slavery to her past oppression to enjoy her freedom with God.

Anastasia was brought up by foster parents, who provided her with much love and care. She never saw her birth parents for the first few years of her life. When her parents did finally show up, she was devastated that she had to leave with two strangers. She was also upset that her foster parents didn't try to keep her. As a result of her childhood experiences, Anastasia had suffered from insecurity all her life. After our prayer, God showed her that when her foster caregivers handed her over to her parents, it was God who carried her in his arms. A sense of peace washed over her, and she knew that God is her unshakable security.

Elise suffered from performance anxiety and would physically shake when she had to speak in front of others. After dealing with some past hurts and rejection, God gave her a vision of being carried by two enormous arms like glowing beams of white light. She drew the picture (reproduced below[9]) and placed it in front of her whenever she had to speak in public. She has since stopped shaking, being reminded of the presence of God with her. May you, too, know the presence of God with you.

9. Unpublished work, used by permission of the artist.

Bibliography

Adams, James E. *War Psalms of the Prince of Peace: Lessons from the Imprecatory Psalms.* Phillipsburg: Presbyterian & Reformed, 1991.

Allen, Leslie C. *Psalms 101–150.* Rev. ed. WBC. Nashville: Thomas Nelson, 2002.

Anderson, A. A. *2 Samuel.* WBC. Dallas: Word, 1989.

———. *Psalms.* Vol. 2, *73–150.* NCB. Grand Rapids: Eerdmans, 1972.

Anderson, Bernhard W. *Contours of Old Testament Theology.* Minneapolis: Fortress, 1999.

———. "Introduction: Mythopoeic and Theological Dimensions of Biblical Creation Faith." In *Creation in the Old Testament,* ed. Bernhard W. Anderson, 1–24. Philadelphia: Fortress, 1984.

Anderson, Neil T. *Victory over Darkness: Realize the Power of Your Identity in Christ.* Rev. and updated ed. Minneapolis: Bethany House, 2000.

———. *Who I Am in Christ: A Devotional.* Minneapolis: Bethany House, 1993.

Arnold, Bill T. *1 & 2 Samuel.* NIVAC. Grand Rapids: Zondervan, 2003.

Arnold, Clinton E. *Exegetical Commentary on the New Testament.* Grand Rapids: Zondervan, 2010.

Augsburger, David W. *Helping People Forgive.* Louisville: Westminster John Knox, 1996.

Bailey, Ken E. *Poet and Peasant and Through Peasant Eyes: A Literary-Cultural Approach to the Parables in Luke.* Grand Rapids: Eerdmans, 1983.

Barker, Kit. *Imprecation as Divine Discourse: Speech Act Theory, Dual Authorship, and Theological Interpretation.* Winona Lake: Eisenbrauns, 2016.

Barnett, Paul. *The Second Epistle to the Corinthians.* NICNT. Grand Rapids: Eerdmans, 1997.

Bash, Anthony. "Difficult Texts: Luke 23.34 and Acts 7.60 – Forgiving the Unrepentant?" *Theology* 119, no. 4 (2016): 276–78.

———. *Just Forgiveness: Exploring the Bible, Weighing the Issues.* London: SPCK, 2011.

Bergen, Robert D. *1, 2 Samuel.* NAC. Nashville: Broadman & Holman, 1996.

Biggar, Nigel. "Forgiveness in the Twentieth Century." In *Forgiveness and Truth: Exploration in Contemporary Theology,* edited by Alistair McFadyen and Marcel Sarot. 181–217. Edinburgh: T&T Clark, 2001.

Blomberg, Craig L. *Matthew.* NAC. Nashville: Broadman & Holman, 1992.

Bock, Darrell L. *Luke 9:51 – 24:53.* BECNT. Grand Rapids: Baker, 1996.

Bonhoeffer, Dietrich. *Psalms: The Prayer Book of the Bible.* Minneapolis: Augsburg, 1970.

Boublil, Alain Albert, Claude Michel Schonberg, Herbet Kretzmer, and Jean Marc Natel. "The Bishop" and "Valjean's Soliloquy." In *Les Misérables: A Musical.* London: Alain Boublil Music; exclusively distributed by H. Leonard, 1998.

Brenner, Athalya. "On the Rivers of Babylon (Psalm 137), or Between Victim and Perpetrator." In *Sanctified Aggression*, edited by Jonneke Bekkenkamp and Yvonne Sherwood, 76–91. London: T&T Clark, 2003.

Brueggemann, Walter. *The Message of the Psalms: A Theological Commentary.* Minneapolis: Augsburg, 1984.

Calvin, John. *Commentaries on the Last Four Books of Moses Arranged in the Form of a Harmony.* Grand Rapids: Eerdmans, 1950.

———. *Commentary on the Book of Psalms.* Vol. 5. Edinburgh: Calvin Translation Society, 1849.

———. *Psalms.* Calvin's Commentaries. Translated by James Anderson. Grand Rapids: Eerdmans, 1949.

Carson, D. A. *Love in Hard Places.* Wheaton: Crossway, 2002.

Cartledge, Tony W. *1 & 2 Samuel.* SHBC. Macon: Smyth & Helwys, 2001.

Chapman, Colin. *Whose Promised Land? The Continuing Crisis over Israel and Palestine.* Grand Rapids: Baker, 2002.

Chilton, Bruce D. "Jesus and the Repentance of E. P. Sanders." *Tyndale Bulletin* 39 (1988): 1–18.

Choo, Maggie Sau Sen. "Generational Sin: An Examination of the Corporate Retribution Formula in Exodus 20:5 in Relation to the 'Sour Grapes' Proverb in Jeremiah 31 and Ezekiel 18." MTh thesis. Regent College, Vancouver, 1999.

Cloud, Henry, and John Townsend. *Boundaries: When to Say Yes, When to Say No to Take Control of Your Life.* Updated and expanded ed. Grand Rapids: Zondervan, 2017.

Collins, Gary R. *Christian Counselling: A Comprehensive Guide.* 3rd ed. Nashville: Thomas Nelson, 2007.

Daube, David. *Studies in Biblical Law.* New York: Cambridge University Press, 1947.

Day, John N. *Crying for Justice: What the Psalms Teach Us about Mercy and Vengeance in an Age of Terrorism.* Leicester: Inter-Varsity Press, 2005.

Dunn, James D. G. *Romans 9–16.* WBC. Dallas: Word, 1988.

Edwards, James R. *The Gospel according to Luke.* PNTC. Grand Rapids: Eerdmans, 2015.

Egwim, Stephen. "Determining the Place of vv. 6–19 in Ps 109: A Case Presentation Analysis." *Ephemerides Theologicae Lovanienses* 80, no. 1 (2004): 112–30.

Elliot, John H. *1 Peter.* AB. New York: Doubleday, 2000.

Enns, Peter. *Exodus.* NIVAC. Grand Rapids: Zondervan, 2000.

Evans, Craig A. *Mark 8:27 – 16:20.* WBC. Nashville: Thomas Nelson, 2001.

Evans, Mary J. *1 and 2 Samuel.* NIBCOT. Peabody: Hendrickson, 2000.

Fee, Gordon. *The First Epistle to the Corinthians.* NICNT. Grand Rapids: Eerdmans, 1987.

Fiddes, Paul. *Past Event and Present Salvation: The Christian Idea of Atonement.* Louisville: Westminster John Knox, 1989.

Fitzmyer, Joseph A. *The Gospel according to Luke X–XXIV.* AB. New York: Doubleday, 1985.

Fox, Michael V. *Proverbs 10–31.* AB. New Haven: Yale University Press, 2009.

France, R. T. *The Gospel of Mark*. NIGTC. Grand Rapids: Eerdmans, 2002.

———. *Matthew*. NICNT. Grand Rapids: Eerdmans, 2007.

Freedman, D. N. *Pottery, Poetry, and Prophecy: Studies in Early Hebrew Poetry*. Winona Lake: Eisenbrauns, 1980.

Garland, David E. *Mark*. NIVAC. Grand Rapids: Zondervan, 1996.

Gerstenberger, Erhard S. *Psalms, Part 2, and Lamentations*. FOTL. Grand Rapids: Eerdmans, 2001.

Goldingay, John. *Psalms*. 3 vols. BCOTWP. Grand Rapids: Baker Academic, 2008.

Gowan, Donald E. *The Bible on Forgiveness*. Eugene: Pickwick, 2010.

Green, Joel B. *The Gospel of Luke*. NICNT. Grand Rapids: Eerdmans, 1997.

Guelich, Robert A. *Mark 1 – 8:26*. WBC. Dallas: Word, 1989.

Gundry, Robert H. *Mark: A Commentary on His Apology for the Cross*. Grand Rapids: Eerdmans, 1993.

———. *Matthew: A Commentary on His Literary and Theological Art*. Grand Rapids: Eerdmans, 1982.

Haber, Joram Graf. *Forgiveness*. Savage: Rowman & Littlefield, 1991.

Hagner, Donald A. *Matthew 1–13*. WBC. Dallas: Word, 1993.

Hamilton, Victor P. *Exodus: An Exegetical Commentary*. Grand Rapids: Baker Academic, 2011.

———. *Genesis 18–50*. NICOT. Grand Rapids: Eerdmans, 1995.

Hankle, Dominick D. "The Therapeutic Implications of the Imprecatory Psalms in the Christian Counseling Setting." *Journal of Psychology and Theology* 38, no. 4 (2010): 275–80.

Harman, Allan M. "The Continuity of the Covenant Curses in the Imprecations of the Psalter." *The Reformed Theological Review* 54 (1995): 66–72.

Hoehner, Harold W. *Ephesians: An Exegetical Commentary*. Grand Rapids: Baker Academic, 2002.

Horsley, Richard A. "Ethics and Exegesis: 'Love Your Enemies' and the Doctrine of Nonviolence." In *The Love of Enemy and Nonretaliation in the New Testament*, edited by Willard M. Swartley, 72–101. Louisville: Westminster John Knox, 1992.

Hossfeld, Frank-Lothar, and Erich Zenger. *Psalms*. 3 vols. Hermeneia. Minneapolis: Fortress, 2011.

Jewett, Robert. *Romans*. Hermeneia. Minneapolis: Augsburg Fortress, 2006.

Johnson, Luke Timothy. *The Letter of James*. AB. New York: Doubleday, 1995.

Jones, Christine Brown. "The Message of the Asaphite Collection and Its Role in the Psalter." In *The Shape and Shaping of the Book of Psalms: The Current State of Scholarship*, edited by Nancy L. Declaisse-Walford, 71–85. Atlanta: SBL, 2014.

Jones, L. Gregory. *Embodying Forgiveness: A Theological Analysis*. Grand Rapids: Eerdmans, 1995.

Kidner, Derek. *Psalms 1–72*. TOTC. Downers Grove: InterVarsity Press, 1975.

Kimmel, Jr., James. "The Nonjustice System (Miracle Court)." Accessed 21 June 2021. http://nebula.wsimg.com/20d34a01f1e4845b0632d3f60c8e724a?AccessKeyId=1 C256BB45AC7AC6816BF&disposition=0&alloworigin=1.

———. *Suing for Peace: A Guide for Resolving Life's Conflicts.* Charlottesville: Hampton Roads, 2004.

Kraft, Charles. *Deep Wounds, Deep Healing: Discovering the Vital Link between Spiritual Warfare and Inner Healing.* Ann Arbor: Servant Publications, 1993.

Landes, George. "Creation and Liberation." In *Creation in the Old Testament,* ed. Bernhard W. Anderson, 135–51. Philadelphia: Fortress, 1984.

Laney, J. Carl. "A Fresh Look at the Imprecatory Psalms." *Bibliotheca Sacra* (1981): 35–45.

Lester, Andrew D. *The Angry Christian: A Theology for Care and Counseling.* Louisville: Westminster John Knox, 2003.

Lewis, C. S. *Reflections on the Psalms.* London: Geoffrey Bles, 1958.

Lincoln, Andrew T. *Ephesians.* WBC. Dallas: Word, 1990.

Linn, Dennis, and Matthew Linn. *Healing Life's Hurts: Healing Memories through the Five Stages of Forgiveness.* New York: Paulist Press, 1978.

Longenecker, Richard N. *The Epistle to the Romans.* NIGTC. Grand Rapids: Eerdmans, 2016.

Longman III, Tremper, and Raymond B. Dillard. *An Introduction to the Old Testament.* 2nd ed. Grand Rapids: Zondervan, 2007.

Low, Maggie. *Mother Zion in Deutero-Isaiah: A Metaphor for Zion Theology.* Studies in Biblical Literature 155. New York: Peter Lang, 2013.

Lucas, Ernest. *Exploring the Old Testament.* Vol. 3, *The Psalms and Wisdom Literature.* London: SPCK, 2004.

Luther, Martin. *What Luther Says: An Anthology.* Compiled by Ewald M. Plass. St. Louis: Concordia, 1959.

Luz, Ulrich. *Matthew 1–7.* A Continental Commentary. Translated by Wilhelm C. Linns. Minneapolis: Fortress, 1989.

———. *Matthew 21–28.* Hermeneia. Minneapolis: Fortress, 2005.

Mackintosh, H. R. *The Christian Experience of Forgiveness.* London: Harper & Brothers, 1927.

Marshall, Julia, Daniel A. Yudkin, and Molly J. Crockett. "Children Punish Third Parties to Satisfy Both Consequentialist and Retributive Motives." *Nature Human Behaviour* 5 (2021): 361–68. https://doi.org/10.1038/s41562-020-00975-9.

Martin, Chalmers. "Imprecations in the Psalms." In *Classical Evangelical Essays in Old Testament Interpretation,* edited by Walter C. Kaiser, 113–32. Grand Rapids: Baker, 1972.

Mathews, Kenneth A. *Genesis.* 2 vols. NAC. Nashville: Broadman & Holman, 2005.

McCarter, Jr., Kyle P. *1 Samuel.* AB. Garden City: Doubleday, 1980.

McKnight, Scot. *The Letter of James.* NICNT. Grand Rapids: Eerdmans, 2011.

Michaels, J. Ramsey. *The Gospel of John.* NICNT. Grand Rapids: Eerdmans, 2010.

Milgrom, Jacob. *Leviticus 1–16*. AB. New York: Doubleday, 1991.

———. *Numbers*. JPS Torah Commentary. Philadelphia: Jewish Publication Society of America, 1989.

Miller, Patrick D. "Syntax and Theology in Genesis XII 3a." *Vetus Testamentum* 34 (1984): 472–76.

Moberly, R. C. *Atonement and Personality*. 1901. Reprint. London: Murray, 1907.

Moo, Douglas J. *The Letter of James*. PNTC. Grand Rapids: Eerdmans, 2000.

Morris, Leon. *The Gospel according to John*. Rev. ed. NICNT. Grand Rapids: Eerdmans, 1995.

Mowinckel, Sigmund. *The Psalms in Israel's Worship*. Vol. 2. Nashville: Abingdon, 1962.

Nehrbass, Daniel Michael. *Praying Curses: The Therapeutic and Preaching Value of the Imprecatory Psalms*. Eugene: Pickwick, 2013.

Nolland, John. *The Gospel of Matthew*. NIGTC. Grand Rapids: Eerdmans, 2005.

———. *Luke*. 3 vols. WBC. Dallas: Word, 1993.

Nystrom, David P. *James*. NIVAC. Grand Rapids: Zondervan, 1997.

Ollenburger, Ben C. *Zion, the City of the Great King: A Theological Symbol of the Jerusalem Cult*. JSOTSup 41. Sheffield: JSOT, 1987.

Peels, H. G. L. *The Vengeance of God: The Meaning of the Root NQM and the Function of the NQM-Texts in the Context of Divine Revelation in the Old Testament*. Oudtestamentische Studiën. Leiden: Brill, 1995.

Piper, John. *"Love Your Enemies": Jesus' Love Command in the Synoptic Gospels and the Early Christian Paraenesis*. Cambridge: Cambridge University Press, 1980.

Poteat, Edwin McNeill. "Exposition Psalms 42–89." In *Interpreter's Bible*. Vol. 4, *Psalms, Proverbs*, 219–486. Nashville: Abingdon, 1955.

Propp, William H. C. *Exodus 19–40*. AB. New York: Doubleday, 2006.

Redlich, Basil. *The Forgiveness of Sins*. Edinburgh: T&T Clark, 1937.

Roberts, J. J. M. *The Bible and the Ancient Near East*. Winona Lake: Eisenbrauns, 2002.

Sailhamer, John H. "Genesis." In *Expositor's Bible Commentary*. Vol. 1, *Genesis–Leviticus*, 21–331. Grand Rapids: Zondervan, 2008.

Saint Augustine. *The City of God*. Translated by Marcus Dod. New York: Modern Library, 1993.

Sakenfeld, K. D. "The Problem of Divine Forgiveness in Numbers 14." *Catholic Biblical Quarterly* 37 (1975): 317–30.

Sanders, E. P. *The Historical Figure of Jesus*. London: Penguin, 1993.

Schmid, H. H. "Creation, Righteousness, and Salvation: 'Creation Theology' as the Broad Horizon of Biblical Theology." In *Creation in the Old Testament*, ed. Bernhard W. Anderson, 102–17. Philadelphia: Fortress, 1984.

Schreiner, Thomas R. *1, 2 Peter, Jude*. NAC. Nashville: Broadman & Holman, 2003.

———. *Romans*. BECNT. Grand Rapids: Baker, 1998.

Seow, C. L. "An Exquisitely Poetic Introduction to the Psalter." *Journal of Biblical Literature* 132, no. 2 (2013): 275–93.

———. *Job 1–21: Interpretation and Commentary*. Illuminations. Grand Rapids: Eerdmans, 2013.

Shepherd, John. "The Place of the Imprecatory Psalms in the Canon of Scripture: Part 2." *Churchman* 111, no. 2 (1997): 110–26.

Simango, Daniel. "Psalms 137." *Old Testament Exegesis* 31, no. 1 (2018): 217–42.

Simango, Daniel, and P. Paul Krüger. "An Overview of the Study of Imprecatory Psalms: Reformed and Evangelical Approaches to the Interpretation of Imprecatory Psalms." *Old Testament Essays* 29, no. 3 (2016): 581–600.

Smedes, Lewis B. *Forgive and Forget: Healing the Hurts We Don't Deserve*. San Francisco: Harper & Row, 1984.

Son, Kiwoong. *Zion Symbolism in Hebrews: Hebrews 12:18–24 as a Hermeneutical Key to the Epistle*. Paternoster Biblical Monographs. Milton Keynes: Paternoster, 2005.

Spurgeon, C. H. *Treasury of David*. Grand Rapids: Baker, 1977.

Stein, Robert H. *Luke*. NAC. Nashville: Broadman & Holman, 1992.

Stott, John R. W. *The Message of Ephesians: God's New Society*. BST. Downers Grove: InterVarsity Press, 1979.

Stuart, Douglas K. *Exodus*. NAC. Nashville: Broadman & Holman, 2006.

Swinburne, Richard. *Responsibility and Atonement*. Oxford: Oxford University Press, 1989.

Tan, Kim Huat. *The Gospel according to Mark*. ABC. Manila: Asia Theological Association, 2011.

———. *The Zion Traditions and the Aims of Jesus*. SNTSMS 91. Cambridge: Cambridge University Press, 1997.

Tran, John C. W. *Authentic Forgiveness: A Biblical Approach*. Carlisle: Langham, 2020.

Tsumura, David Toshio. *1 Samuel*. NICOT. Grand Rapids: Eerdmans, 2007.

Tucker, Jr., W. Dennis, and Jamie A. Grant, *Psalms*. Vol. 2. NIVAC. Grand Rapids: Zondervan, 2018.

Vaught, Carl G. *The Sermon on the Mount: A Theological Investigation*. Rev. ed. Waco: Baylor University Press, 2001.

Villanueva, Federico G. *It's OK to Be Not OK: Preaching the Lament Psalms*. Carlisle: Langham Preaching Resources, 2017.

Volf, Miroslav. *Exclusion and Embrace: A Theological Exploration of Identity, Otherness, and Reconciliation*. Nashville: Abingdon, 1996.

———. *Free of Charge: Giving and Forgiving in a Culture Stripped of Grace; The Archbishop's Official 2006 Lent Book*. Grand Rapids: Zondervan, 2005.

Vos, Johannes G. "The Ethical Problem of the Imprecatory Psalms." *Westminster Theological Journal* 4 (1942): 123–38.

Wallace, Daniel B. "ΟΡΓΙ'ΖΕΣΘΕ in Ephesians 4:26: Command or Condition?" *Criswell Theological Review* 3, no. 2 (1989): 353–72.

Waltke, Bruce K. *The Book of Proverbs Chapters 15–31*. NICOT. Grand Rapids: Eerdmans, 2005.

Weaver, Dorothy Jean. "Transforming Nonresistance: From *Lex Talionis* to 'Do Not Resist the Evil One.'" In *The Love of Enemy and Nonretaliation in the New Testament*, edited by Willard M. Swartley, 32–71. Louisville: Westminster John Knox, 1992.

Wenham, G. J. *The Book of Leviticus*. NICOT. Grand Rapids: Eerdmans, 1979.

———. *Genesis 1–15*. WBC. Waco: Word, 1987.

Wesley, John. *The Works of John Wesley*. Grand Rapids: Zondervan, 1958.

Wilkins, Michael J. *Matthew*. NIVAC. Grand Rapids: Zondervan, 2004.

Wink, Walter. "Neither Passivity Nor Violence: Jesus' Third Way (Matt. 5:38–42 par.)." In *The Love of Enemy and Nonretaliation in the New Testament*, edited by Willard M. Swartley, 102–25. Louisville: Westminster John Knox, 1992.

Wolterstorff, Nicholas. *Justice in Love*. Emory University Studies in Law and Religion. Grand Rapids: Eerdmans, 2011.

Worthington, Everett L. *A Just Forgiveness: Responsible Healing without Excusing Injustice*. Downers Grove: InterVarsity Press, 2009.

Worthington, Everett L., ed. *Dimensions of Forgiveness: Psychological Research and Theological Perspectives*. Philadelphia: Templeton Foundation Press, 1998.

Wright, David P. "Ritual Analogy in Psalm 109." *Journal of Biblical Literature* 113, no. 3 (1994): 385–404.

Zenger, Erich. *A God of Vengeance? Understand the Psalms of Divine Wrath*. Louisville: Westminster John Knox, 1996.

Zerbe, Gordon. "Paul's Ethic of Nonretaliation and Peace." In *The Love of Enemy and Nonretaliation in the New Testament*, edited by Willard M. Swartley, 177–222. Louisville: Westminster John Knox, 1992.

Scripture Index

NEW TESTAMENT

Langham Literature and its imprints are a ministry of Langham Partnership.

Langham Partnership is a global fellowship working in pursuit of the vision God entrusted to its founder John Stott –

to facilitate the growth of the church in maturity and Christ-likeness through raising the standards of biblical preaching and teaching.

Our vision is to see churches in the Majority World equipped for mission and growing to maturity in Christ through the ministry of pastors and leaders who believe, teach and live by the word of God.

Our mission is to strengthen the ministry of the word of God through:
- nurturing national movements for biblical preaching
- fostering the creation and distribution of evangelical literature
- enhancing evangelical theological education

especially in countries where churches are under-resourced.

Our ministry

Langham Preaching partners with national leaders to nurture indigenous biblical preaching movements for pastors and lay preachers all around the world. With the support of a team of trainers from many countries, a multi-level programme of seminars provides practical training, and is followed by a programme for training local facilitators. Local preachers' groups and national and regional networks ensure continuity and ongoing development, seeking to build vigorous movements committed to Bible exposition.

Langham Literature provides Majority World preachers, scholars and seminary libraries with evangelical books and electronic resources through publishing and distribution, grants and discounts. The programme also fosters the creation of indigenous evangelical books in many languages, through writer's grants, strengthening local evangelical publishing houses, and investment in major regional literature projects, such as one volume Bible commentaries like *The Africa Bible Commentary* and *The South Asia Bible Commentary*.

Langham Scholars provides financial support for evangelical doctoral students from the Majority World so that, when they return home, they may train pastors and other Christian leaders with sound, biblical and theological teaching. This programme equips those who equip others. Langham Scholars also works in partnership with Majority World seminaries in strengthening evangelical theological education. A growing number of Langham Scholars study in high quality doctoral programmes in the Majority World itself. As well as teaching the next generation of pastors, graduated Langham Scholars exercise significant influence through their writing and leadership.

To learn more about Langham Partnership and the work we do visit **langham.org**

CPSIA information can be obtained
at www.ICGtesting.com
Printed in the USA
BVHW091047260123
657203BV00014B/378

9 781839 736858